HOW THE MARKET MAKERS EXTRACT MILLIONS OF DOLLARS A DAY AND HOW TO GRAB YOUR SHARE

A TRADING METHOD THAT YOU CAN APPLY TODAY FOR IMMEDIATE RESULTS

MARTIN COLE

***

HOW THE MARKET MAKERS EXTRACT MILLIONS OF
DOLLARS A DAY AND HOW TO GRAB YOUR SHARE
by
Martin Cole

INTRODUCTION

The cafe was buzzing the minestrone great, my table shot to the left and the soup exited on the right. The culprit, an expensive suit apologized and ordered me another.

I tried a conversation with his colleague; it was soon clear that conversation was not on the cards. I admit I was eavesdropping; I had to, they were talking about the markets and trading was not going well for me.

I was about to try my luck at gleaning some information when one suit said to the other.

> "OK, so ...,you do not act today in one, you assist if needed, and that's all. Blue will be setting up from 2-3:30 news at 2.30 you step in at about 46 and pick up the stragglers, OK?"

The other suit nodded in agreement and then they drifted off into talking about boats and my courage to interrupt faded.

I decided to go and see the London Stock Exchange building before heading back home. I got lost on the way, but eventually, I was standing in front of the building when I heard a familiar voice. I turned to see Mr. Minestrone, as I now like to call him.

He looked right at me with a twisted expression that turned to a glare as he brushed past. He looked at me again over his shoulder as he entered the LSE building.

That was the last time I ever saw Mr. Minestrone. Although I didn't realize it at the time, he was to be the most influential person I ever met regarding trading. Several years would pass before the overheard conversation of Mr. Minestrone would change my life forever.

Warning! What you are about to read is going to shock you. For certain, many of your currently held beliefs about how markets work are going to be left in tatters. You are about to discover the real market, a market that few traders ever get to understand and I estimate less than 1% of the general public have a notion of.

Corruption, misdirection, and manipulation are the ingredients of the great murder mysteries novels. The financial markets contain the same ingredients.

This book is for the trader who has tried the systems, the patterns, the indicators and the strategies. It's for the trader who has paid for expensive training courses and $97.00 for the trading 'secrets.'

This book is for the trader who has concluded that something is wrong with trading. It's for the trader ready to get off the merry go round of madness and start making money.

ALSO BY MARTIN COLE

THE BILLIONAIRE AND THE BACKPACKER

Imagine starting your life over again but with all the life experience of today.

It would be a dizzying journey of success and achievement that would leave those around you standing in awe.

They would have no clue where your wisdom, foresight, and abilities came from. A sought-after person you would be for sure.

The Billionaire and the backpacker story is inspired by true events. The messages woven through the story will reveal to you the potential for a restart - a reboot of your life. It's a book that could quite possibly change your life!

The billionaire and the backpack takes you on a captivating journey from the sidewalks of New York to the Peruvian jungle where an ancient ceremony revealed that nothing is without meaning, consequence and maybe even destiny.

Take this book home tonight and expose yourself to the very real possibility of a life-changing story.

Copyright © 2011 Martin Cole

All Rights Reserved. No part of this publication may be reproduced, stored in a retrieval system, or transmitted, in any form or by any means, electronic, mechanical, photocopying, recording, or otherwise, without the prior written permission of MJC Training Trust Ltd.

Latest revision of this book September 2017

— MARTIN COLE

DEDICATION

For Denise My wife, my best friend and mother of our two wonderful adventurous sons Steven and James. Having you all by my side always makes me feel like the richest man on the planet.

Martin Cole.

HOW I BECAME A TRADER

In 1990. I was declared a bankrupt. That event left me homeless with two young children and a wife to take care of. We had no alternative but to live in a 13ft caravan (Caravan = Trailer if you're an American cousin) which we shared with rodents. We were desperate but did not want to show this to our sons, so we convinced them that we were all on an adventure. To this day (near 30 years on) both our sons remember and talk fondly of our 'adventure.'

Looking back this was not a pleasant time in life, but it was certainly character building. Given the subject of this book, you could be forgiven for thinking that it was trading that caused my bankruptcy. But the truth is that I had not even discovered trading at that time.

In fact, I was so naive over financial markets that I had not managed to work out that rising interest rates had cut the money supply to my business. It was these interest rates that had placed me in the bankruptcy court.

Today things are very different. Today, I enjoy the luxury of living a comfortable lifestyle in several different countries. At the time of writing this, I am aged 59 years and live in the spectacular South Island New Zealand.

I wasn't born into a life of this privilege. For me, the road to prosperity has been a long and winding one.

The third of six children, I grew up on a small farm in the village of Towcester in Northamptonshire, England.

While never an academic child, I was bright "He can turn his hand to anything" was the comment people used to make. I have certainly turned my hand to plenty of activities over the years.

While I didn't discover for a long time that my strength lay in trading, I always felt I going to do something unusual with my life. I had a deep sense that I was capable of much more than I seemed to be achieving.

I met my lovely wife when she was sixteen and a half and I almost as young. I knew straight away she was the one for me. She didn't realize so quickly, though, and stood me up three times before we finally went out on our first date! We got married when we were eighteen and twenty. She has supported me in everything I have done, through difficult times, bankruptcy, success and everything in between. Her philosophy has always been: "Go for it. If you don't, you might regret it."

We have two wonderful sons and Denise is even more beautiful now than she was all those years ago. Even if I had not managed to achieve financial freedom, having her by my side would have made me a wealthy man by default.

I started in business in the building industry, meeting with some success until the British economy collapsed – along with my order book. In that year – 1990. There was a 75 per cent increase in bankruptcies in the area where we lived. We lost our house, our lifestyle, the lot and were left with no choice but to live in that 13ft caravan with our two small boys, Steven and James.

I went to work with my father and Denise took a range of menial jobs to make ends meet. Between us and with the help of a close friend, we saved up enough money to open a pizza delivery business. We kept on our day jobs and made pizzas at night.

Those were difficult times. Our sons were little more than babies. We would put them to sleep upstairs above the kitchen and take them home, still sleeping, at one or two in the morning, before getting up again to start another day.

The pressure the situation put on our little family was horrendous. We kept going for fourteen months until we managed to sell the business and make a small profit. We needed a break from everything so we headed off to Greece, with the idea we might be able to find something to do there and get out of the rat race.

Greece is a beautiful country, but without an occupation, I was sitting in front of our rented house doing nothing but contemplate the view and my rapidly increasing waistline! After about three months we realized we were not doing the right thing, and returned to England, harsh reality, hard work, and winter.

One day I picked up on a copper trading scandal that was making waves in the news. At around the same time, I got an unsolicited mailing in the post, advertising a trading course. Something clicked in my mind, and I felt sure this could be a good way to escape all the hassles and problems of a traditional business.

I spent a couple of months trying to get a handle on the business of trading. I knew nothing about the technical side of things – I had never even seen a live chart on a screen and didn't know anything existed like that. I was trying to learn from newspaper articles until I realized that what I was doing was not practical for turning this into a successful business. I still needed a lot more information.

My first contacts in the industry told me about data feeds and other technical details, but I wasn't informed enough to know exactly what I needed. Eventually, I got in touch with a broker in London. He asked me what I knew about trading and suggested I get in touch with a gentleman who was offering training. I completed a course with him over some weekends. It was theoretical with little practical use, but as I had no reference point with which to judge, I wasn't aware of the course's discrepancies. Nonetheless, the course introduced me to the world of trading, and I have no regrets for having taken it.

After completing the course, I decided to sell the business in which I was then involved, making a profit of twelve thousand pounds. I invested this in a data feed, software and some capital for my broker's account. In the first six weeks, I made six and a half thousand pounds profit and thought I'd found Utopia! It was incredible.

Reality struck quickly. However, I soon I found myself just holding my own. I was winning and losing, but all the time I was steadily being relieved of my money. Then things started to go horribly wrong, and my stress levels were affecting not only me but also my wife and children. I reached the point where I felt everything was against me. The market was against me. The world was against me.

No matter what trading indicators I used I was failing spectacularly. My personal best was when I managed to carry out thirty-two losing trades in succession! Yes, you read that right thirty-two in succession!

How could that be even possible? I mean if you flicked a coin could you do that bad? No, you could not so what was going on?
　　Later on, as we get further into this, you will learn exactly how it was that I could achieve the incredible consistency of those losing trades.

The thirty-two losing trades was my turning point. Those losses gave me the opportunity to understand two critical aspects of trading.

Firstly I recognized the failures were in part being generated by myself because of the fear I had built up around trading. Trading had become very stressful. The human mind will do what it can to get you as far away from anything that it deems dangerous. Fight or flight as the saying goes. My subconscious was trying to remove me from a stressful occupation.

A sure way to eliminate a trader from trading is by removing his or her money from their possession. If you have no money to trade with, then you have no choice, but to leave the market. I believed I was going to lose and my belief became a self-fulfilling reality. Mission accomplished by the human psyche. I was removed from the trading (stressful) environment.

I stopped trading for a while and spent some time analyzing myself and other peoples' trading practices. I became fascinated by the way peoples' beliefs affect their lives. And how a person will hold onto a belief even in the face of contrary evidence. In many cases holding a belief until new evidence is so compelling that the belief comes tumbling down in a mess. After the mess, they are forced to take up on the new belief that the factual evidence provided.

Note*

Factual evidence may be just as flawed and thus give rise to an entirely illogical new belief. Now, even with further evidence, this new belief will be defended until it goes through the death - birth cycle that all changed beliefs go through.

I then had a major shift in market perspective. While before I had visualized the market as a sort of free-floating entity, I now saw it as a sea of people. Rather than changing prices, a sea of indecision and fear. I now saw it as an ocean of ever changing beliefs about future price.

Think about beliefs for a moment.

A trader will not press the buy button on his/her dealing platform until he/she 'believes' that stock will increase in value. Likewise, a trader will not sell a stock unless there is belief that it will fall in value and thus take something from him if he continues to hold that stock.

This is a fundamental TRUTH about ALL trading decisions. All trading decisions are based on what a trader BELIEVES about future price. This simple fact is so crucial as you will soon discover.

With my new understanding, I started trading again, and something remarkable happened.

I now understood at the back of every trading decision was a belief. I reasoned that if I could read these beliefs, then I could read the market and predict the future of stock, commodities or foreign currency.

Now there were no gambles, but steady earning. I managed to hold onto most of my gains, and I made sure losses were minimised. I was also trading much less than I had done before, once or twice a day, and sometimes as little as once or twice a week. As my account grew, so did my confidence, but I still felt there as 'something' still not quite right. I felt there was another part of this story that had to yet reveal itself.

Then, destiny stepped in the form of Alex Whitcombe, a computer technician whom I contacted for help with a broken computer. When he opened my machine, he recognized there was trading equipment installed, and we started to talk.

As our friendship developed, Alex would come and watch me trade, and shortly after, I approached him with a proposal. I wanted to get my concept of trading beliefs to trade turned into a software program.

I carried on trading, and Alex started to develop his programming skills. As his expertise grew, we worked together creating a software package for mapping the market. None of the earlier attempts were successful, but we kept plugging away at it.

I started looking at market beliefs as they were manifested within a single day's trading. I was trying to identify the days when it seemed likely I was going to lose money so that I could avoid trading during those times. Later on, I realized that most traders look for trading opportunities whereas I was looking for when NOT to trade. (I told you I was pretty green at this stage)

My success in identifying "no-trade" days paid off and did wonders for my account. I was trading less and earning more.

I continued working with Alex, and between us, we produced a piece of software which we called "Bright Futures."

A journalist investigated the program and discovered it worked eight times out of ten. This is an extraordinary success for any trading software. The journalist wrote up a story about it which you can read on my website: www.learningtotrade.com

But still, I felt 'something' was eluding me. I could not get into the big time and start making serious profits. Every time I stepped up to trade, I still had a nagging feeling all was not as displayed. I felt like every time I looked at a chart on a computer screen I was staring into a shop window, a shop window that had been prepared for me in some way.

I ignored my nagging doubts and dived in the deep end.

IMPORTANT NOTE

In reviews of an earlier edition of this book, I have been criticised for using the book to sell the reader my trading software. Not only was this untrue but it did massive damage to the reader because just when they started to understand the method. They developed a mistaken belief that my software was required to trade the method.

I categorically state that you DO NOT NEED my trading software to trade this method. The METHOD exists INDEPENDENT of ANY software or indicator.

My software is my 'choice' of a TOOL to use. It is not the choice of all of my students. In fact, about 50% of my students do not use my software.

A BAD TRADING DAY

I had had a particularly bad time of it recently; my 'dive in action' had resulted in my trading account being almost empty again. I remember, head in hands, repeating over and over "It's a bloody mess."

The sense of desperation and confusion was completely overwhelming. If I didn't stop what I was doing, I was likely to lose everything.

During this time I was working out of a converted stable on my fathers' small farm and on his way to tend the animals, he popped his head around the door. He caught me with my head in my hands.

"What's up?"

"Oh nothing, I just can't seem to crack this business."

He looked at my computer screen for a moment and said.

"My father always used to say, money and corruption, where you find a lot of money, you will often find corruption."

My father left to tend the animals as I continued staring at the computer screen.

A few moments later my mind invited in Mr. Minestrone. There I was, thrust back in time to the cafe where again I heard the words.

"OK so today, you do not act today in one, you assist if needed that's all. Blue will be setting up from 1.30 to news release at 2.30 you step in at about 46 and pick up the stragglers, and away we go OK?"

It is said when the student is ready, the teacher appears. Well, I was ready, and the financial markets were about to become my greatest teacher.

Within a very short time following that message from my subconscious, I was well on my way to financial freedom.

I had left England and was living on the Costa del Sol in Spain. Today as I am writing these words I am aged 52 years, semi retired and living in the South Island New Zealand. From my perspective life at this time doesn't get any better than this.

I am going to reveal through the following pages how overhearing a conversation, led me to discover something that exists within financial markets. Something that is there for the benefit of the few to the detriment of the rest of us.

I used this information to secure financial freedom for myself, and I truly believe armed with the information therein, you can do the same.

Why tell my story now?

I had been considering revealing this information for some time, but a tight fishing line has always proved to be a pull from the keyboard. After all, there is always tomorrow to tell the story.

But something has happened. Something that I predicted would happen when the corrupt nature of markets was discovered. I did not envisage that this would happen in my lifetime, but it seems like it may be under way.

The Occupy Wall Street movement started. The common man is suspicious, he senses something is wrong with the system.

Of course, the movement may die or become conveniently annexed from the media. However, what will remain is a nagging doubt, a remembrance of the event until something fires it all off again. I remain confident in the prediction that after some difficult years we will see a world wide change in monetary and ownership policy. This change will provide a much fairer world in the future.

However, it will not be without the loss of life as the power brokers try to maintain control of the lives of the masses for their benefit.

By taking the contents of this book and carving out your financial future, you will be taking nothing from the common man. You will instead be reclaiming that which has been taken from you. That which is still being taken from you, by way of the consummate greed of those controlling financial markets.

Well, it's time to make a start, it's time to reveal what Mr. Minestrone was planning that day and how the same plan will be carried out tomorrow.

IT'S NATURAL FOR YOU TO WANT TO BE A TRADER

Trading - the exchange of goods between individual people or institutions is as old as human society itself. Today it exists among all groups of individuals, from complex, technological societies to small-scale groups still living in the Stone Age.

The exchange of valued items has been the impetus behind every imperialistic movement, irrespective of ethnicity.
 European societies (including the British, the Spanish and the Dutch) colonized Africa, the Americas, parts of Asia and elsewhere, to have access to goods with which to trade.

All around the world, peoples from the Aztec to the Zulu have developed social relations, conquered and been defeated to further commercial interests.

The history of human existence is, to a considerable extent, the history of trading. The question of access to material goods has been behind most alliances as it has wars, it has been the reason for strategic marriages between important families and the inspiration of many religious practices. It is part of what and who we are.

The hunter-gatherer's exchange of a bow and arrow for another useful item may seem to be very different to the buying and selling in a modern marketplace, but the impulses behind the deal are the same. Keep this in mind as we progress.

The modern trader must never forget the qualities of "use" and "value" are very subjective. If a social group (or an individual) believes that an object is valuable, then, effectively, it is. The belief in use or value of an object is the impetus behind the sale rather than the object's actual value. If indeed "actual value" can even be said to exist at all.

Trading remains the driving force behind national and international relationships. To an extent, the failure or success of governments and alliances is determined by important actors in the trading sphere.

Thanks to the increasing accessibility of technology, and the fact that trading is conducted increasingly on the Internet, it is possible for many people from different backgrounds and educational backgrounds to enter the market as independent traders.

People sometimes ask me, "What type of person becomes a trader?" – And there is no straightforward answer. There is not a "traders personality"; there are, however, informed prepared traders and uninformed traders.

This book is for two groups of people. Those who have never traded and wish to start off on the right foot. Those who have already experimented with trading, with less than satisfactory results.

The overall aim of this book is to turn you into an informed and powerful trader. This contents of this book are the keys for you enjoy financial freedom for yourself and your family.

Most trading books concentrate on the "visual how-to" elements of the business. They attempt to show you charts and indicators, and for the most part, this type of book is very popular. The reason for the popularity is because of the COMMONLY held BELIEF that trading success will be found in a PATTERN on a chart or a 'secret' INDICATOR.

If you BELIEVE the pattern and indicator myth and refuse to accept any 'challenge' to this BELIEF, then you will at the end of this book become deflated. You will then likely go back to looking for something to support your BELIEF in patterns.

If you are not seeking a PATTERN or INDICATOR but rather a METHOD that NEVER changes and offers consistent rewards you will be empowered. You will have something that less than 5% of the traders in the world today understand.

Let's make a start.

We will be examining not only the basics of the market and trading but also an element which is at least as important. The impact your personality, your subconscious and the people around you have on your trading performance.

People are not machines, but emotive beings – not a bad thing in itself, but a factor that has to be monitored and controlled in an environment that makes no allowances for a bad day. Awareness of one's potential strengths and weaknesses is the first and most important step in launching oneself into the market.

It is my goal to help you to know yourself better and, in doing so, to become a successful trader. My aim in creating this book is to bring to you the advice I wish I had, had at hand when I started trading, and to help you to avoid the mistakes I made.

This book is to reveal to you 'the market makers method. The method is the market makers business model. It is this business model that we are going to explore.

This is a trading method that has succeeded, not only for me but also for those with whom I have shared it. What is more important, as you will soon come to discover. This is a trading method that never changes, a system that once learned can be applied to any market you wish to trade.

The most important attitude to bring to any new enterprise is optimism, mixed with just the right amount of humility. You should have a willingness to learn. You should approach this method with an open mind and be ready to challenge, not only your conception of what trading is all about but also your preconceptions about yourself. You may find this experience more rewarding than you can currently imagine.

1

THE MARKETS AS A BUSINESS

A word of warning! What you are about to read is possibly going to shock you. For certain, many of your currently held beliefs about how markets work are going to be left in tatters. You are about to discover the real market, a market that few traders ever get to completely understand and I estimate less than 1% of the general public have a notion of.

UNTRUTHS, corruption, misdirection, and manipulation are the contents of the great murder mysteries novels. The financial markets contain the same ingredients.

MAKE NO MISTAKE; the markets are a highly efficient business with strict rules that are 100% profit driven.

LET'S take a look inside the market makers business and explore how we as informed traders can become part of THEIR business.

Trading Truisms

Truism is a word I mention frequently as we get further into the book. For this reason, I think it wise that I define for you exactly what I am inferring when I use this word and also explain how important it will prove to be when your trading live.

I DID a quick dictionary check on the the word 'truism, ' and this is what came back

'COMMONPLACE, cliché, hackneyed/trite/banal/overworked saying, stock phrase, banality, old chestnut, bromide; maxim, axiom.'

AS YOU CAN SEE it's pretty hard to nail down the exact meaning, but I think it's fair to say that the word conjures up the feeling of something of dubious value. Certainly, something you would maybe better looking into before you took decisive action and or commitment.

TRADING TRUISMS ARE BENIGNLY dangerous to your trading wealth. They creep up on you in times of heightened awareness (stress - anxiety) and offer temporary relief to distract you from actions that need to be taken now

THE PROBLEM from a trading perspective and truisms is how they remove focus from the here and now and offer hope for the future. Hope and future being the operative two words in this sentence.

- 'The trend is your friend.'
- 'The chart doesn't lie.'
- 'Stops always protect you.'

- 'The news drives the market.'

The list of these truisms is exhaustive so rather than me try to cover them all here I can provide you with a way to guard against them.

TRADING TRUISMS ARE at their most deceptive and dangerous just before you enter a market and also while you are in the market with open positions. For this reason, you must become attuned to them and their effect on you.

FOR OUR PURPOSE whenever I mention the word 'truism' I am conveying the dubious nature of the thought, image or action that it might trigger.

LET'S TRY AN EXAMPLE.

YOU HAVE an open position in XYZ stock. The stock has been trending up. You have studied and are well versed in the market makers method. Suddenly something triggers your attention. You sense that good times are coming to an end. You look at the shape of the chart, and you see the trend is all up. The thought 'the trend is your friend' comes to mind, and you loose the 'something' that triggered your attention.

WHAT JUST HAPPENED IS that a truism that has no basis, in fact, has influenced you. You may move up your stop-loss, you may check the news you may look a little closer at your charts, but the fact is a truism has removed your connectivity and control of your future and placed it with something of dubious nature.

So how do you guard against something that is often of very subtle nature?

You remain vigilant for the interference to your first thought, feeling or sensation regarding your (in this case)XYZ stock.) I can't place this 'feeling' into the written word, neither can it be handed to you. However, you already KNOW this feeling. You have experienced it many times before, especially if you have been trading for any period.

I am not giving you something new here, some secret weapon. I am only bringing to your attention that which you may have discarded so many times that it is now a weakling of its former self. Don't worry; this weakling will bounce right back once you start to give it some attention.

So, now we understand what a truism is (our definition) and how to spot them affecting your trading let's move onto something that every trader needs in order to succeed.

CONSISTENCY

Consistency is vital for traders. Without the ability to repeat profitable results, we would be winning one minute and then giving it away the next.

However, for now, I want to lead you away from individual trader consistency and talk about the consistency of the market makers.

We are looking at the markets as a business entity - not our business but the business of the market makers. The market makers' business has rules, very defined rules, which are governed by the desire and absolute need for profit.

Many view markets differently. You will often hear statements along the line of:

"The markets are there for the benefit of everyone."

"It's a free market and driven by supply and demand."
"The markets are too big to be manipulated."

These statements are designed to mislead the outside traders. They are truisms, and they are self-perpetuating. (The most powerful truisms are self-perpetuating)

The consistency that you are learning about here is based on the absolute need for the market makers to produce a profit. The profit that ultimately pays for the towering office blocks and the greed and power lust of the market makers themselves. Take one city tower block in any financial capital in the world and then take a wild guess at hour by hour running costs. Then multiply that by huge numbers of tower blocks with ever increasing costs, and you might begin to merely scratch the surface of the amount of money being swallowed up on a moment by moment basis.

This money that has to be extracted from financial markets on a daily basis.

As a side note here while I am mentioning tower blocks. Next time you are in even the smallest of towns look for old buildings that are built of quality and costly materials (in their day) In New Zealand it's extremely clear to see the names on these buildings. They are always Banks or Insurance / Mutual Societies.

Due to this inescapable need for profit seeking, we can be assured the market makers actions are always motivated by that need, along with personal greed for ever increasing profits. Profits which can only ultimately come from the working class (don't you just hate human labels). The working class is where the real value to society is, it's where it's always been.

Given these monetary needs, it would be naive in its extreme to believe this need would be left to chance? It would be naive to believe that these vast empires of financial wealth did not have a repeatable business plan, like any other business, in the pursuit of profits.

I think we would have little trouble in agreeing that the way to produce a profit from trading at a base level, is to buy something at a given price and then later sell that at a higher price; or sell something at a given price and then later buy it back at a lower price.

Both of these actions will create profit. Both of these actions are the activities of every trader and at the same time, the market makers. We can see traders are in competition with the market makers on every level.

If the successful trader is taking money out of the coffers of the market makers, why do they allow you to 'sometimes' make fairly easy profits?

For a trader to buy or sell, we are forced to do business with the market makers on their terms (orders may be placed through an online broker, but ultimately everything leads back to the market makers).

For a trader to buy anything, the market maker must supply the sell to match the buy.

If a market maker is willing to sell to you at a 'bargain' price and since the market maker has a vested interest in making a profit, we can at least believe that he has done the math and is not going to sell you something that he knows you are going to make money on, and which he is going to lose money on.

Let's get back to consistency

I have reduced this to the most basic level of a single transaction, solely to explain the business plan of the market makers at the root level. When not reduced to this level, it's difficult to place everything into perspective. What we need is to amplify this single transaction into hundreds of thousands of transactions every day. This continuous cycle of buying and selling, and selling and buying, gives us our first consistency factor.

The second level of consistency is the methods they use to generate their profits. The market makers use the same methods day in, day out, to achieve their aim. By trading the market makers business model, you are assured your trading model will be consistent.

The third level is the consistency of supply and demand. You may have the best widget in the world, but if there is no demand for it, then you are not going to be able to sell it.

In the markets, however, supply and demand is not nearly so straight forward.

IDEALISED SUPPLY AND DEMAND

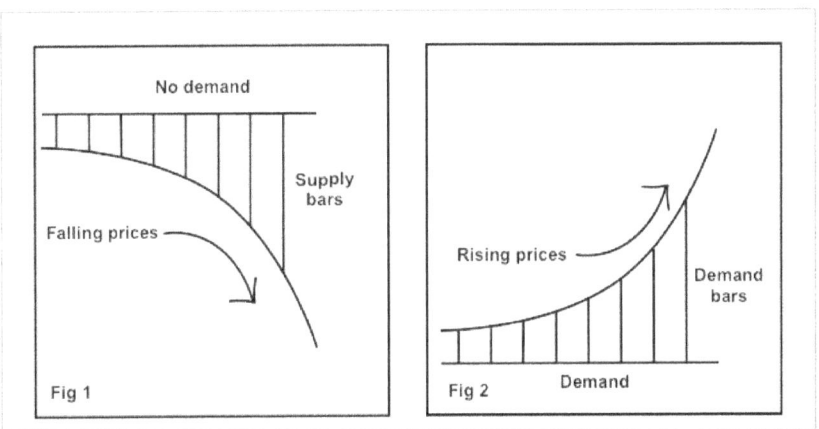

The two diagrams above illustrate an idealized view of supply and demand.

In Fig 1 the price of the stock is falling in alignment with supply. As supply increases without demand, the price will fall equal to the supply bars to the angle of descent. Fig 2 shows the opposite; prices are rising with equal demand. Together, these images illustrate the public's perception of the market, where supply and demand are matched in a simplistic manner. The truth is that the reality of supply and demand is never that straightforward in financial markets.

MARKET MAKERS SUPPLY AND DEMAND

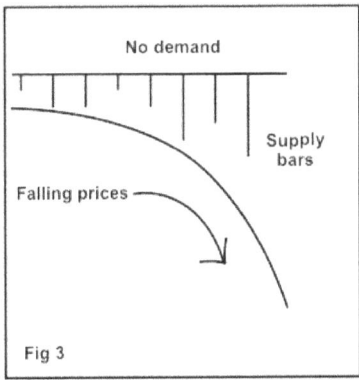
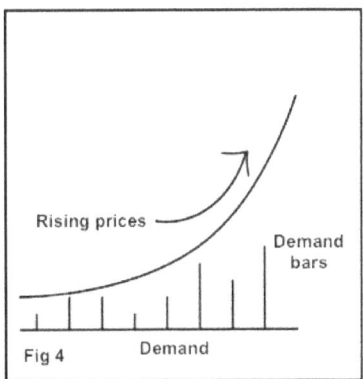

Figs 3 and 4 are a far more accurate illustration of supply and demand in the financial markets environment.

These illustrations are showing that prices can be manipulated away from the genuine supply and demand curve. Prices become detached from the truth of genuine supply and demand and are given momentum by manipulation.

This manipulation is a fundamental component in the market makers business. We will examine this manipulation in greater detail as we get further into the book.

So far you have been introduced to market basics along with a brief look at two types of supply and demand. One genuine and one manipulated.

We will be returning to supply and demand, but for now, we need to sidestep to examine the movement of stock and prices.

THE CIRCULARITY OF STOCK MOVEMENT

Your ability to consistently profit from trading financial markets will be directly linked to your ability first to develop and then maintain an insiders perception. You will need to think like and act like a market maker.

You will need to work within the business model of the market makers. (market makers are the insiders) While working within the market makers business model, you will need to be constantly aware of the outsider's perception. (The outsiders are the general public) You need a foot, in both camps as they saying goes. In our case, however, we need the perception in both camps.

The outside perception of markets are the images presented to us on charts and many televised news reports. Those wavy rising and falling lines we see as back drops to the news readers create that impression of what markets look like and how they move. The truth is, the markets are not like this at all. They are in fact completely circular. See Fig 5

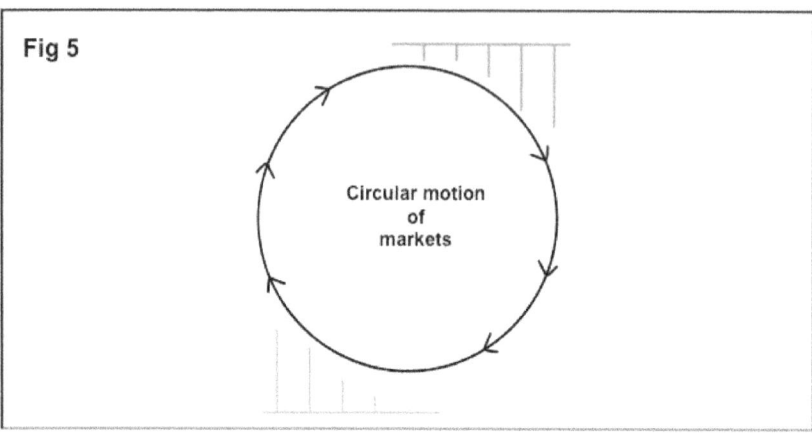

Fig 5 — Circular motion of markets

While this circularity applies to all markets, the explanation of this circularity is more easily explained using the stock of an individual company.

The circular nature of stock is inevitable because the amount of stock issued is finite. Market makers cannot just generate fresh stock in a company; they must work with the limited amount of material (shares) that the company has issued.

The rising and falling lines on charts only show half of the story. They show the visible outcome of price movement. The circular motion reveals the inner workings of the market makers business.

The way the market makers work the stock is by buying and selling. Buying and selling creates the peaks and troughs of the wavy lines that outsiders see illustrated in charts.

Insiders and profitable traders view and understand the market from a very different and much more accurate view.

As you look at fig 6 keep in mind the limited supply of any one stock.

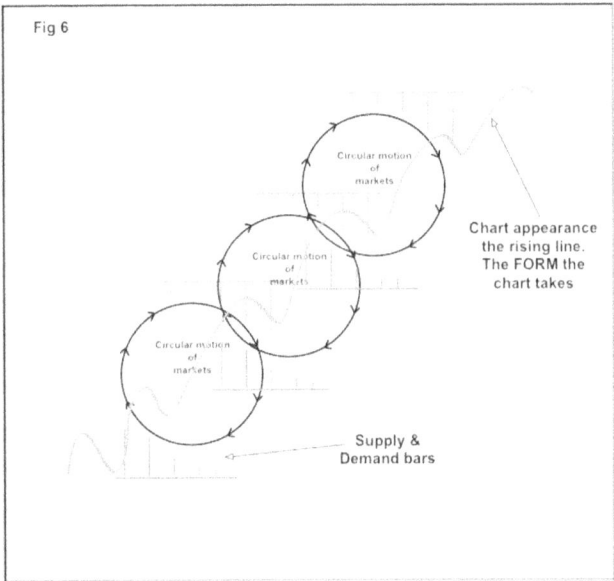

Here in Fig 6, we have three copies of the circle that we saw in Fig 5. Running through the circles is a rising and falling line. The rising and falling line represents an overall rising stock, albeit with occasional downturns.

The rising and falling line is what the outsiders see as a tradable stock.

Now is the time to bring in the important subject of FORM and CONTENT.

The rising and falling line in the overall up trend of this stock in fig 6 is showing us the FORM or shape of the stock as prices rise and drop back before rising again.

FORM is the shape of the chart. FORM provides us with very

little information. This FORM the chart takes is what most traders trade. Most traders look for 'patterns' in the FORM and then REACT to those patterns.

Oh, how the human mind LOVES patterns. The mind wants to patternize everything, so when that pattern repeats we are instantly, subconsciously instructed to act accordingly. Patterns do not have to be images of course. Audio patterns affect us in the same way.

Back to our stock example

As the supply of any one stock is limited, the only way for you or I to buy any of that stock is for someone to sell it to us Stock cannot be magically conjured out of thin air. There must be an exchange.

Question:
Why would anyone sell a stock that is continually rising in value?

They wouldn't However, if the price of that stock moves down, this may encourage some traders to take the profits the stock has already provided. The only way they can release those profits is if they liquidate their stock. I.e. they SELL that stock to a willing BUYER.

Remember that this sale and purchase has at the back of it one very important human trait. You will hear a lot about this trait throughout the book and it's something you will have to continually ask yourself while trading. (I'll get to that trait in a moment)

First, let's break down that sale and purchase.

The seller believed the stock was unlikely to go higher so decided to sell and take his/her profits.

The buyer believed that the price was going to go higher, so he/she bought.

So what was the ONE factor behind this transaction that was the same for both seller and buyer?

The human 'trait' of BELIEF decision making.

Both traders were able to engage in this transaction because they had DEVELOPED BELIEFS about the future. This has nothing to do with PRICE. Price is a RESULT of traders beliefs NOT the CAUSE of them.

That is so fundamental to your success that I must repeat it.

Price is a RESULT of traders beliefs NOT the CAUSE of them.

More still, will sell their stock for fear of any down turn continuing. Negative news, poor reports, can all be used to mark a stock's value down and encourage selling.

Encouraging selling by doing what?

By creating BELIEFS about the future.

The market makers create supply and demand by creating BELIEFS about the future. Market makers do not manipulate the price; they don't need to. Traders do that all by themselves when they act on their BELIEFS about future price.

Let's look at the mechanics of this.

As traders develop beliefs and act on those beliefs (assuming in this case the beliefs are that the value of this stock falls further) more and more traders will want to get out of this stock.
 Let us call this falling stock RED company stock.
 Let us also create an imaginary stock called BLUE.
 Blue stock has just had some positive publicity. Traders are looking at the FORM of the chart, and they see the price rising.
 The FORM of the chart creates a BELIEF in higher prices in the future and transactions to BUY BLUE take place.

As increasing amounts of the perceived poor value red stock are sold, the market makers can start to buy this stock. They are ACCUMULATING the red stock for later use.
 Later use will be when the market makers have accumulated all the available red stock and then through FORM again convince traders to now BUY.

The CYCLE of buying and selling has taken place, and the largest of consistent profits goes to the market makers.

The very act of ACCUMULATION by the market makers withdraws the accumulated stock from the market, and it makes it more difficult to obtain. Something more difficult to obtain rises in value. Now, with a little promotion of this red stock, demand for it increases, and the prices are now marked up.

As demand for this stock increases, the market makers are now able to sell that which they accumulated as the price was falling.

Thus, the circle of ACCUMULATION and then PROFIT RELEASE is accomplished as the stock the market makers accumulated while the price was falling is later promoted by creating BELIEFS in higher future prices. RED stock turns to blue and BLUE to RED and so on, continually. This is the circularity of stock movement. Circularity is the CONTENT of the market. CONTENT is the truth of the market. FORM (the shape of the chart) hides the content.

Now multiply this circularity of stock into say, the FTSE 100 index or the DOW, and you will begin to understand the vast and yet simple workings of an overall market index. There are thousands of different company stocks all cycling through the never ending circle of accumulation, profit release, accumulation, ad infinitum.

The market makers do all they can to hide this CONTENT and promote outsiders to view the markets as simplistic supply and demand, thus keeping true manipulated market activity hidden from view.

The outsiders market view is the view of the chart, the appearance, the form the chart takes. The market makers do not want the outsiders to see which stock is being accumulated and which stock is being sold back to investors after the accumulation process.

If everybody understood the reasons behind rising and falling stock prices, the market makers would lose their position of power and their simple business would become very difficult to operate.

Probably about now, you are asking yourself how you can ever hope to become a successful trader, without being privy to the financial muscle or information that the market makers have.

Well, here is what will determine your success.

As a trader, you are by definition on the outside of the market, when compared to the market maker. To become a successful trader, you have to use the best tools at your disposal. In short, your brain and your knowledge of how market makers function.

To trade like a professional, you have to be able to think the way the market makers think. You need to be able to look at the market from the inside; you have to concentrate on the content of the market makers business model.

In addition to this.

You must learn to understand how traders act and react to market conditions. This understanding will give you a depth of insight comparable to the market makers. The good news is that by the end of this book, you will have this understanding and the skills required.

Keep in mind that if you understand within YOURSELF how YOUR BELIEFS work, then you will understand how others work. (This is the only part of trading psychology you need - despite thousands of gurus telling you that trading is all psychology)

When you look at markets with a view to taking a trading position (buying or selling), you must continually be asking

What beliefs are being created?
    What beliefs are being challenged."
    Where is a belief SHIFT likely to happen relative to the market/stock that I am looking at now.

Now we need to get back and examine the foundation of this solution so that you have a solid grounding in the market makers method.

2

ELEMENTS OF THE MARKET MAKERS BUSINESS MODEL

ACCUMULATION

To better understand accumulation, let us draw on an analogy of an apple orchard owner who has to stock his market stall tomorrow to sell his apples. Should he pick his apples for one hour or two? Should he pick all the apples today and take them all to market? The best course of action for our orchardist is to pick that which he knows he can sell and leave the rest for another day.

The next day he might asses demand differently and pick accordingly. He might be able to pick fast if one tree is holding a dense crop or it may take longer if several trees have light crops.

What we can draw from this is:

1. Quantity is going to be influenced by demand.
2. The time taken to accumulate is going to be governed by the ease or difficulty in which he can accumulate all the apples he wants.

RETURNING TO THE MARKET MAKER, we can see that he is in the same situation as our orchardist. The market maker will complete his accumulation according to the anticipated demand, and his accumulation time will depend upon the difficulty or ease in which he can do this.

I cannot over emphasize the importance of understanding and remembering these two accumulation factors.

LET'S now look at what the FORM of accumulation looks like.

Careful! Remember the difference between FORM and CONTENT

Accumulation areas

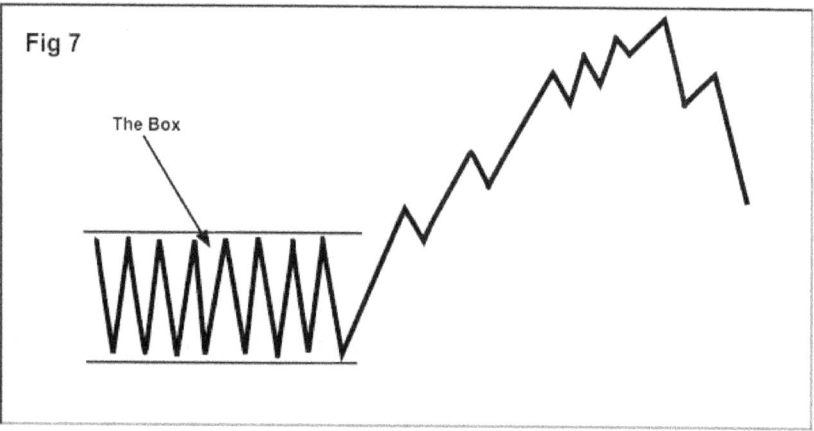

In Fig 7 you can see that I have highlighted an area and labeled it the box. From now on, we are going to interchangeably reference the accumulation area by also calling it "the box'. This will give us a much faster way to bring our attention to it during a further discussion and distinguish it from other areas of accumulation. You might find it useful to think of this box as our orchardist box he is filling with apples.

Let us now examine the elements of accumulation individually.

NOTE: While the accumulation area often has the appearance of a uniformed box rarely will it fit neatly into such confines. The term 'box' allows us to quickly draw attention to an area of the chart that is important for the trader to understand.

THE ACCUMULATION CYCLE

There is a phrase often quoted 'perception and reality.' I believe there is no place more appropriate for this phrase than financial markets, and the activity of accumulation fits this phrase like a glove.

The perception of an accumulation cycle is due to a trading truism, and as we now know, these truisms are often used to assist in the creation of traders beliefs. We also know that these truisms are often accepted as real truth by the majority of traders, regardless of supporting evidence. They are accepted as truth because they APPEAR through FORM as if they ought to be true.

Truisms are perpetuated because they serve a purpose for the market makers.

The truism in the case of an accumulation cycle is that its CONGESTION.

The word congestion, when used by a trader, seems to explain well a tight range of prices displayed on a market chart. This is the perception - it looks right, it appears this way, and it is shaped like a box.

Not only is this description incorrect but it also prevents us from digging deeper into why this area on the chart has appeared.

The reality is this congestion is a covert operation of either, the accumulation of buy orders or accumulation of sell orders.

Note*

    Buy orders are also known as long positions and sell orders as short positions

Given the fact that the market maker has instant access to information we do not, we can draw a logical conclusion that he can at any time:,

Assess with a high degree of accuracy whether the outside traders are favorable to either higher or lower price.

He can also create market sentiment for either direction, based upon his overall information.

Once the market maker has discovered or manipulated the most desirable overall future market direction, he can then plan to accumulate either buy orders or sell orders, from which he will later release profits. However, this accumulation must be done in such a way as to not reveal which side of the market he is accumulating. He must run a covert operation.

A COVERT ACCUMULATION PLAN

The entire accumulation cycle must be hidden from view. If it were not, then the market maker would not be able to accumulate successfully.

To better understand this, imagine for a moment you are the market maker, and you wish to accumulate BUY orders to later sell at a higher price.

If you were to advertise this fact, this would not encourage outside traders to sell to you, in fact quite the opposite would occur. What we would see by looking at the form of the chart is something as in Fig 8

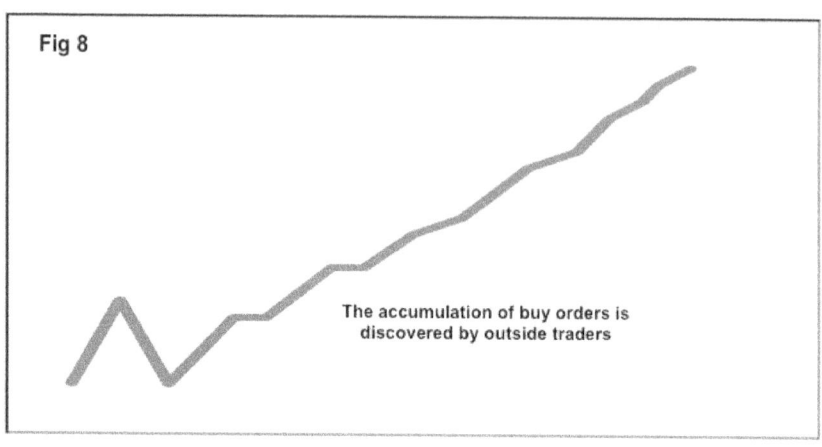

Fig 8

The accumulation of buy orders is discovered by outside traders

What the market makers would end up with would be a situation where the outside traders would be buying with them; this would have the effect of almost instantly increasing prices. Any accumulation planned by the market makers will have failed. Thus they will not be able to accumulate stock to sell later at higher prices and so generate profits.

During the accumulation cycle, there must not be a showing of any intention as to which side of the market the market maker is accumulating.

This deception is achieved by the market maker marking the prices up and down, within a tight range. This tight range will take on the chart form resembling a box like shape. The box like shape is only the form of the chart and bears no reflection to what is actually happening within it. Remember FORM and CONTENT

During this accumulation phase, the market makers create conflicting beliefs so that their hidden buying or selling will not be discovered.

Note* Buying or selling will depend on whether they know the market is going to go up or down when the accumulation phase is complete)

DIRECTIONAL BELIEFS

Keeping prices in a tight range satisfies another criterion, which is that beliefs will not be developed by the outside traders regarding any one particular direction when the market eventually breaks free of the confines of the box like formation.

The trader's inability to develop a belief about future direction causes a state of mind in the outside traders of conflict and confusion. This conflict and confusion will also be used by the market maker to reach out and quickly grab large amounts of buy or sell orders (depending upon which side he is accumulating)

This conflict and confusion cause a CONDITIONED RESPONSE by many outside traders. This conditioned response initiates the setting up of trading orders either side of the box like area.
    This type of position taking is an attempt to profit when the market eventually breaks free of this box like area either up or down.
    This method of trading is often called breakout trading or break from congestion trading. This is another one of those misleading

trading statements. It is NOT congestion. Congestion is the FORM the chart is taking. The FORM is not the CONTENT of what is really going on.

Note* Trading orders placed either side of a market are either buy or sell orders to be actioned immediately or later under conditions attached to that order.

This breakout truism has the perspective of being a wise thing to do and is often heavily promoted as part of; or a complete standalone trading strategy. However, the reality of trading like this will mean that you are playing a virtual slot machine and regardless of you catching breaking moves, you will lose money over time.

The market maker uses this break out strategy and the resulting confusion to his advantage. Let us now have a look at how this works against the trader and for the benefit of the market maker.

ACCUMULATION BY WAY OF TRADERS BREAKOUT ORDERS

The breakout trading method promotes the placing of orders either side of what traders assume is congestion. Trades placed in this way allow the market makers to trigger orders that they wish to accumulate. Fig 9

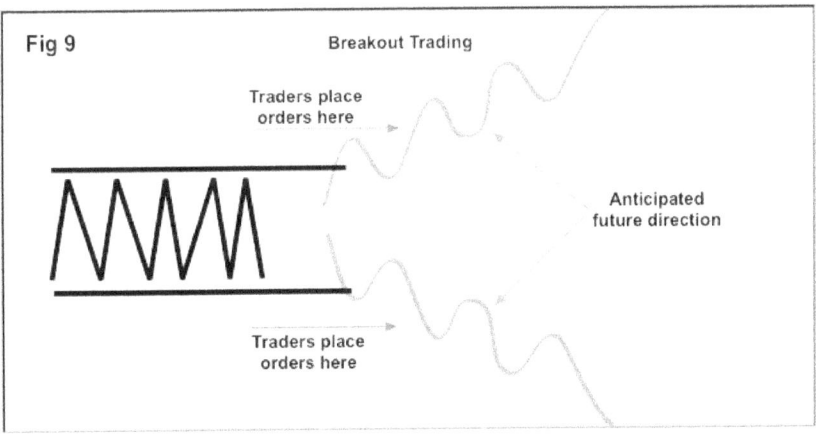

Let us look at this in practice.

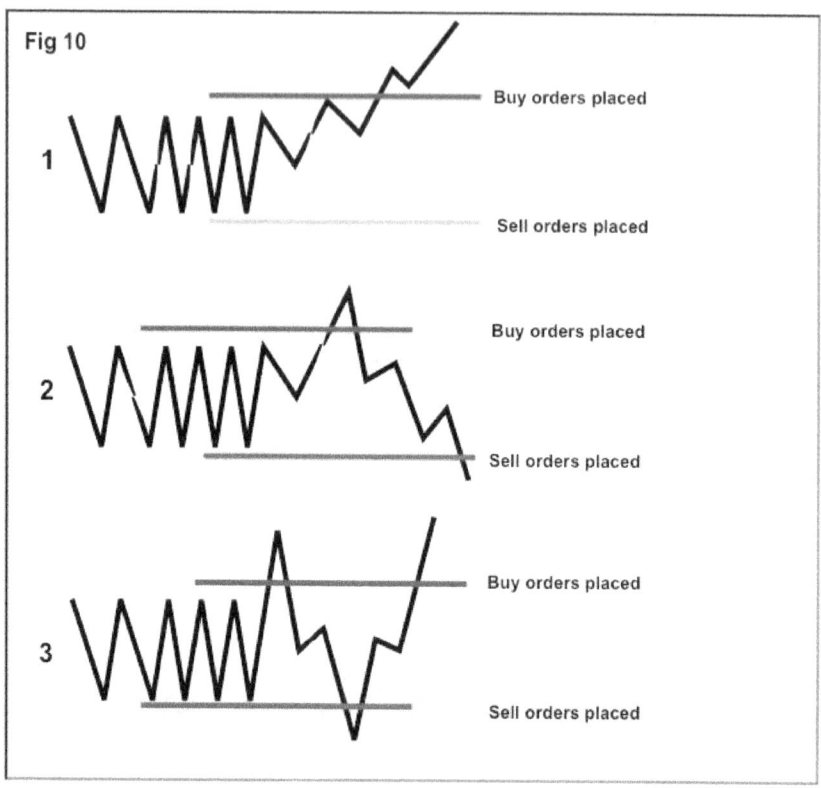

Fig 10

In Fig 10 example 1, the market moves up and triggers the buy orders where outside traders have placed them. The market move continues up and has the potential of a successful trade for the trader.

In Fig 10 example 2, the market moves up and triggers the buy orders where outside traders have placed them, but rather than continuing upwards, the market falls and now triggers any sell orders placed.

The traders whose orders were triggered when the market first moved to the upside, would have placed sell stop orders to protect themselves from open ended loss. These traders would have placed sell stops and as the market moves lower, these orders would have been triggered, resulting in losses for the traders who had bought on the first move up.

In Fig 10 example 3, the market moves up triggering the buy orders, then triggers the sell orders, then again triggers the buy orders.

The traders caught in example 3 generally suffer heavy losses and are often too 'shell shocked' to continue trading at this point and thus miss any subsequent profitable move. This type of market movement is often called 'whipsaw'; this is another trading explanation that offers no real insight as to what is really going on. The purpose of this type of move by the market makers is one of rapid accumulation whilst creating maximum confusion and fear.

As you can see from these examples breakout trading seems like a good idea; it sounds plausible to simply place orders either side of a market and then wait for it to break.

This type of trading is encouraged and promoted by the market makers and is readily accepted by many traders.

Breakout trading is another form of accumulation for the market makers to use as and when they have been unable to accumulate the desired amount whilst the market was trading in the tight accumulation range.

What defines the desired amount of accumulated buy or sell orders is the amount the market makers believe they can later release profit from. They will not accumulate more orders than they believe they can later release for profit.

STOPLOSS ORDERS

The word stop loss holds the connotation that it will stop or limit your losses. In part this is true, and one should never trade without a stop loss order in place. However, stop loss orders are also one of the tools of the market makers.

We now know from our earlier discussion that a primary part of the market makers business is accumulation. Like our orchardist, if you have not accumulated your apples from the tree, then you can't take them to market.

We also know the market maker is always going to try to accumulate all he wants or rather all he knows can be taken to the end result of releasing profits.

The stop loss order is an excellent tool for the market maker, and he will use it whenever he has the desire to increase his accumulation amount.

A trade consists of two sides, so if a market maker wants to accumulate buy orders, then he will need to create the belief in the wider market that the market is likely to fall rather than rise. As traders start to believe this, they will be less likely to want to buy the market and will favor selling.

When these traders sell, the market makers will take the other side - they are buying, they are taking the other side of the sell order. They are accumulating buy orders.

Conversely, if a market maker wants to accumulate sell orders, then he will need to create the belief in the wider market that the market is likely to rise rather than fall. As traders start to believe this, they will be less likely to want to sell the market and will favor buying.

When these traders buy, the market makers will take the other side - they are selling, they are taking the other side of the buy order. They are accumulating sell orders.

Where stop loss orders are placed

It is highly predictable where traders will place stop loss orders.

Stop loss orders will be placed at:

- Even number price levels
- Recent price reactions
- Published areas of support or resistance

Traders will also place mental stop loss orders in an attempt to hide from the market makers where they will close their trade.

Note* Mental stop loss orders are prices that traders hold in their heads as they are looking at a market chart. They will be saying to themselves "I will hold this trade unless it reaches X price" (x price being a price they have mentally set).

ROUNDED NUMBER PRICE LEVELS

Rounded number price levels are often used by inexperienced traders, who are under stress as they are trading. Under stress, the human mind will always take the path of least resistance. It is a lot easier for the mind to just jump to a price such as 1.5600 than it is to think about 1.5873. Market makers are well aware of this, and this is why one will often see markets retrace from their overall trend back to rounded, numbers before then continuing in the overall direction of the trend again.

∼

Think about this as we go into this next section

RECENT PRICE REACTIONS

Fig 11 Recent price reactions are favorites with most traders. The reason for this is because they LOOK like they should work. The FORM the chart takes gives the appearance a price has moved either up or down to a certain price and retraced from there to then continue its overall directional trend.

Traders will conclude that as the market found support at these retrace levels, it is unlikely to return to this level; thus any stop loss placed here is likely to be in a safe zone, allowing the trader who had earlier bought the market to make profits from the continuing rise.

Stop loss orders placed like this, offer high potential for market makers accumulation, should they wish to fill up or add to their desired accumulation quota.

Note* Support and resistance are common traders terms which are more truisms. Support and resistance are accumulation areas.

Let's have a look at how market makers use outside traders stop loss orders for accumulation.

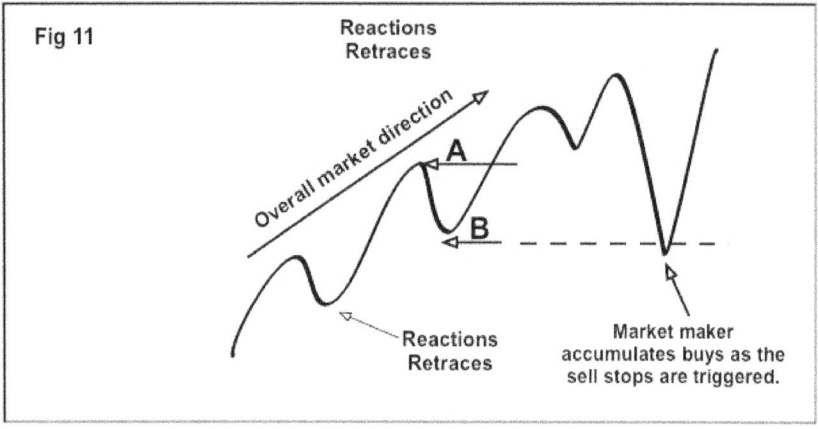

In Fig 11 as the market moves above the peak at (A), traders will place stop loss orders at the base of the retrace (B). Should the market maker want to accumulate more buy orders to sell higher, all he has to do is drive the market down below the level of (B) which will trigger traders sell stops; the sell stops are quickly bought by the market makers causing an immediate and rapid rise to continue the overall trend.

Placing stop loss orders like this will sometimes work out for the trader and steady gains will be made, until the market makers wants to accumulate some more orders at which time the trader will fall victim to manipulation. This is why trailing stop loss orders APPEAR to be a great way to maximise profits, but this is just another truism perpetuated by the market makers. It's a very clever accumulation tactic.

PUBLISHED AREAS OF SUPPORT AND RESISTANCE

Market makers release news about where they say major support and resistance levels are. One will often hear news statements like "We believe XYZ price to be a significant support level for the market, and as long as the market stays above this, investors are likely to remain positive."

The advantage for the market maker releasing this type of information and then what it prompts traders to do concerning the placing of stops should be self-evident.

As we can see, the common stop loss as it is known is a very powerful market makers tool which is used with impunity against traders. However, there is no need for despondency because, given this knowledge, it can be used to the informed trader's great advantage.

Understanding WHY, WHEN and WHERE traders place stop loss orders allows the informed trader to view things from the market makers perspective.

Once you can anticipate where stops are likely to be in large numbers and see the market makers harvest those stops you will have little doubt whether they are accumulating buy or sell orders. Given the knowledge of the accumulation of buy or sell orders, you will be able to predict the resulting future market direction with remarkable efficiency.

∽

Just read that above paragraph again, please.

∽

I hope at this stage you can see how that one paragraph defines you looking at the CONTENT of the market and not the FORM or SHAPE of the chart.

3
INTRODUCING THE MARKET MAKERS BUSINESS MODEL

By this stage, you should now have a solid understanding that the markets are akin to a shop window, which is 'dressed' for traders to shop in, and this shop window is manipulated over time with different displays as chart patterns. You will also have learned that the financial markets are a business whose sole purpose is to produce profits for the business owners, the market makers.

WE ARE NOW GOING to examine the market makers business in much closer detail, so you can learn first the correct way to observe and then how to profit.

HOW TRADING INFORMATION IS PRESENTED

Trading information is presented to us as charts, that is we are presented with a series of graphic images, which purportedly offer us insight into a stream of numerical figures. This simple and yet vital transition is often completely overlooked by many traders as they forget what market data is, and instead focus on these graphic images. Graphic images are as you now know the FORM the chart takes.

You might like to think of this as looking at a shop window or through a shop window. Looking at a window we see the surface of the glass, looking through the glass we are no longer aware of the glass, and our attention has shifted to what lies beyond the glass.
    When traders are looking at chart patterns, they are looking at the glass, not through it. Looking at the glass, the trader's vision is obscured and does not have the depth of vision required to trade successfully.

FORM AND CONTENT

Yes I know I have mentioned this before, but now I want to explain this in greater depth so bear with me and pretend I have not mentioned it up until this point.

Form and Content. These two words are essential to understanding how to read ALL financial markets.

When we talk about content, we mean the market makers business model. This consists of both a setup phase and the profit release phase. This CONTENT IS ALWAYS THE SAME but the form it takes on the chart is many and varied.

In other words, the content can appear in many different forms on the chart, but it is still the one content of accumulation and then profit release.

I am not saying every time the market makers cycle of manipulation occurs; it will appear on the chart in a discernible way; what I am suggesting is that it will appear enough times in a discernible way, for us to make profits on a regular basis. However, it will only appear discernible to a person who is practiced in the market makers business model.

The main skill is to be able to perceive the accumulation and manipulation cycle, using the many and varied forms it takes on the live chart. Sometimes the manipulation cycle is obviously very discernible in a chart; however, most times it is only discernible to a practiced eye.

It might help here to clarify by further example what I mean by form and content.

Let us take the definition of a circle. A circle is an enclosed curved line, alike in every particular, every point of which is an equal distance to the point in the center.

This is a very accurate statement of content. This is content we can UNDERSTAND in our minds, although it is not something we can see with our senses until it takes form as a sensible object.

I could draw a big circle, a small circle, a purple circle or a yellow circle. It won't matter. If I understand what a circle is, I will recognize it in any form it takes. Circles can come in many forms. In other words, the form is what we can see with our eyes.

Now an interesting point here is that even if the form of the circle is not complete, it can still clearly indicate the content. This fact is very important for those of you who are learning this method of trading. It is important because even though many times the form the manipulation cycle is taking on the chart is not complete, it will still clearly indicate to a trained eye the content. In this case, the mind fills in the gaps. In our case, the knowledge of the market makers business model allows us to fill in the gaps and enter the market.

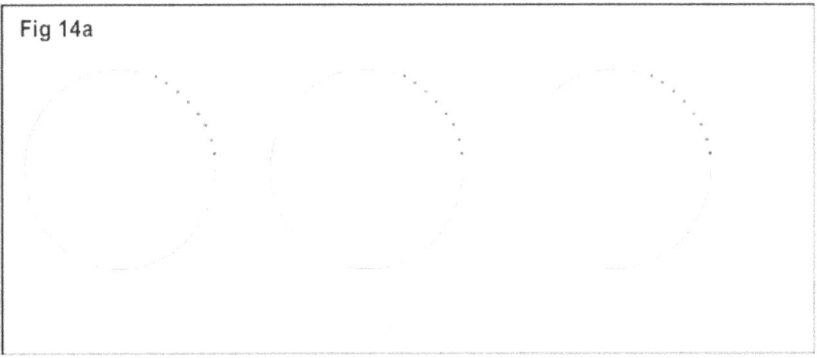

Fig 14a

As you can see, in Fig 14a there are many ways to indicate a circle quite clearly, even though regarding form there are big gaps. However, with a thorough understanding of what a circle is, the mind can easily fill in the gaps, and a circle can be clearly discerned.

The reason I am making this point is that you can never know BEFOREHAND what the form of a chart will look like. This does not matter, however, because it is the mind's recognition which is the important factor, not what the chart looks like in form.

In earlier illustrations, I needed to show you examples of the form, and at the beginning, these examples had to be clear and obvious. The reason for this was so you could begin to get a sense of how the content we are interested in takes a particular form on a chart.

The main point I am trying to make here is we are not trying to learn chart patterns from which we can predict market moves. Rather, we are looking at the market makers business model the chart is presenting, and seeing if we can discern what phase it is in and what which side of the market is being accumulated.

Once your mind is practiced in this approach, you will look at the chart, and your mind will automatically fill in the gaps and discern where the market makers are in their cycle of accumulation, manipulation and profit release. This will become clearly evident, even if the chart "look" or form is one you have never seen before.

I don't want you to think of chart patterns. I want you to think of the market makers business model, and practice recognizing it being played out using the chart.

When you are well practiced in this, your mind will have the necessary skill of looking at a chart, and without any logical process involved, you will be able to spontaneously discern the model. When you can rely on yourself and your understanding to determine your trading activity, your trading will move to an entirely different level. You will be free from trying to make sense of lagging technical indicators wrapped in truisms.

SKILLS TO TRADE THE MARKET MAKERS MODEL

There are several important skills to learn to succeed in trading the market makers business model, but the two most important are:

1. A thorough understanding of what is going on behind the FORM of the charts.
2. Self-observation. (Self-observation enhances your skill in reading how the masses are thinking)

The thorough understanding is achieved by learning the market makers business model and how this functions (the purpose of this book).

Self-observation involves learning and then developing the skill to quickly detect whether you are on the outside looking at the shape of the chart, or on the inside observing the market makers activity.

Number two may seem like a simple task but the effort required for constant self-observation is intense, and if one's guard is dropped for very long the risk of being removed from inner observation to the outer rises quickly.

The moment you are moved to outer observation (the outer being the form of the chart on your screen) the charts start to take on life and meaning that is being PRESENTED to you by the market makers.

This transformation from the inner to the outer generates thoughts and feelings leading towards decision making that will be flawed.

Self-observation is the process of monitoring one's perspective and listening to one's inner conversations, to spot early signs that you are being drawn to chart analysis and not content analysis.

There are subtle clues that you are wavering from the required content path.

Amongst these are:

- Focussing in individual bars
- Comparing one bar to its immediate predecessor
- Becoming fixated on a chart pattern
- Ignoring earlier price activity in favor of now activity
- Watching the live price of the market continually change

The greatest teacher for learning self-observation will be yourself as you experience these sensations and thus become aware of them.

THE THREE PHASES OF THE MARKET MAKERS BUSINESS MODEL

The three phases of the market makers business model will always happen in sequence. There may be an occasional deviation if profit making opportunities present themselves, but the phases will fall naturally back into sequence.

It is this continual repeatable sequence which offers the great advantage over traditional technical analysis trading methods.

Note*The deviation would not be a move from one phase to another; rather it would be the extending of the first or second phase.

Phase one

The first phase of the market makers business model is either the accumulating of BUY orders or the accumulating of SELL orders.

If buy orders are being accumulated, the market makers will be later moving the market to higher prices; conversely, if the accumulation of sell orders is taking place then the market will later be moving to lower prices.

These directional moves, relative to what is being accumulated, are inescapable facts and provide what I call a default market move that you can profit from.

Once you discover which side of the market is being accumulated, you will profit by default.

The accumulation BUY cycle

The purpose of the buying cycle is for the market maker to accumulate BUY orders, the only way this can be achieved if they convince a proportion of traders to SELL to them

How this proportion will be persuaded to sell will be explained in greater detail later on, but briefly, for now, they will sell to the market maker if they believe the market is going to fall, either now or sometime in the future.

The accumulation SELL cycle

The purpose of this cycle is for the market maker to accumulate SELL orders, the only way this can be achieved is if they convince a proportion of traders to BUY from him.

How this proportion will be persuaded to buy will again be explained in greater detail later on, briefly, they will be willing to buy from the market maker if they believe the market is going to rise, either now or some time in the future.

You will notice what must be more than a 90% similarity of the two most recent paragraphs. This similarity was not an oversight, but rather to impress the small but significant differences between them.

A quick jump forward in time. (Remember we will return to the 'how' of the above)

Phase one completion

Phase one of the set up is complete when the market maker has achieved his desired quota of buy or sell orders. Buy or Sell orders will be depending on which way the market is going to be taken, either up or down.

In the case of an accumulation of buy orders, we can be confident the major part of any move from the accumulation area will be going up. Like wise, we can be confident in the case of an accumulation of sell orders that the major part of any resulting market move will be down.

Phase two

The second phase of the market makers business cycle is one of manipulation. However, this manipulation phase also blends into phase one.

For a clearer understanding, we will separate this manipulation into two distinct market maker desired outcomes.

1. Manipulation to accumulate.
2. Manipulation to wrong foot traders at the most opportune time, to rapidly accumulate.

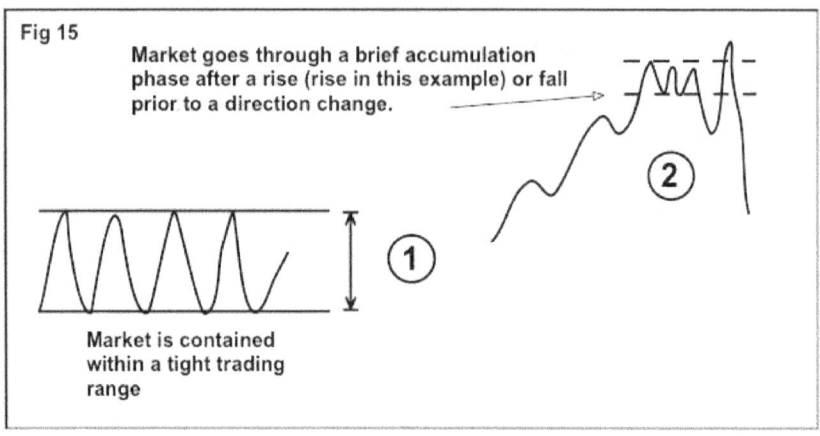

Fig 15

Market goes through a brief accumulation phase after a rise (rise in this example) or fall prior to a direction change.

Market is contained within a tight trading range

Manipulation to accumulate is carried out by holding the market in a fairly consistent shape, (1) This shape we call the 'box'; however, it is important to remember that when you are thinking of this as a box, you are not just looking for a shape. There is also accumulation at the point of market makers; targeting traders stop loss orders (2)

In fig 15 we can see two different market shapes and yet they are intertwined, as they are both parts of the accumulation phase. The utmost diagram in Fig 15 has an element of stop taking to add to the accumulation.

Rules of manipulation to accumulate

1. Covert operation
2. No discernible direction
3. No desire to create predominate beliefs

The accumulation cycle is always a covert operation. Failure to keep hidden whether the market maker is running an accumulation of buys operation, or an accumulation of sells operation, will jeopardize the second phase for them.

It is challenging to decipher with 100% consistency which side of the market is being accumulated while within the box like shape. However, this is of little importance because just like the poker player with the most expressionless face, eventually the player (in this case the market maker) will be forced to show his hand. It is this showing of his hand which presents to us the opportunity to join the market maker on his inevitable journey to either higher or lower price.

As a brief example here which will be covered in depth further on. The 'showing' of the market makers hand can often be clearly seen by monitoring when and how the market makers run a stop accumulation move.

By discerning if a stop running move is accumulating buy or sell stops, one can determine what the content of the main body of accumulation is. If a market maker has been accumulating buy orders, then any stop running exercise to accumulate more will by default be organized to accumulate more of the same. When trading the market makers business model, stop takes are not to be feared, they are to be welcomed for the future potential they reveal.

No discernible direction

There can be no discernible direction during the accumulation phase. This is achieved by keeping the range of the market within tight confines. This tight range is, by the outside masses, given the label of 'congestion.'

This word, as you already know while highly descriptive, is very also deceptive. Congestion implies nothing is happening, a little like sitting in a traffic jam creating apathy and boredom.

At this point, it is worth highlighting again the idea of form and content relative to the word congestion. If the trader looks at this area of the chart and defines this a congestion area, then the trader is looking at the form the chart is taking and not the content.

No predominant beliefs

The avoidance of creating predominant beliefs in the outside market is paramount. This is achieved by moving the market up and down at a slow rate and in a tight range. During this period, traders will be unlikely to develop beliefs in any one particular direction at the expense of another. This allows the market makers to continue accumulating the side of the market they desire, without significantly extending the price range and creating pre-determined beliefs.

MANIPULATION TO WRONG FOOT TRADERS

Manipulation to wrong foot traders will generally take place when 90% of the desired accumulation quantity has been achieved. The method is simple and yet devastatingly effective, to conclude phases one and two.

The set up for this wrong footing starts in phase one; however, this is not something the market makers actively do as a separate phase as they have already created confusion within the masses.

This confusion creates a mindset in the trader that is fueled with a trading truism around breakout trading. Breakout trading is where traders try to capture a move as the market breaks from the truism of congestion.

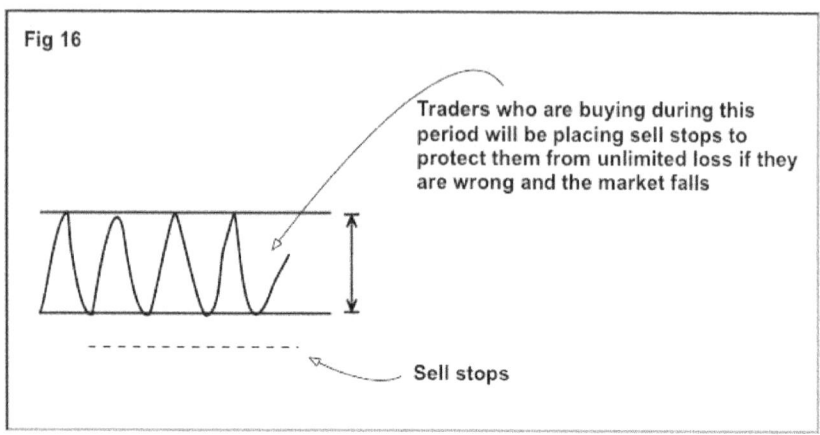

As the market makers move the price up and down within the tight confines, traders will early on take trades according to their beliefs at that time. For ease of explanation, we will assume in this instance the market makers are accumulating buy orders for a later rising market.

Gradually, as time extends, other traders will also start to accumulate buy orders in the same area.

During the accumulation phase, the outside traders who are also accumulating buy orders will be placing stop loss orders to protect themselves in the event of the market falling. These stop-loss orders will be placed at and around proximity to recent ranges (see Fig 16).

The longer the accumulation process continues, the more nervous and jittery the outside traders become, and the closer in they will move their stop loss orders, in an attempt to limit potential losses.

Keep in mind that the trader group we are discussing here are the group who are at this stage buying with the market markers, albeit they are not aware of this liaison.

The market makers are aware of these stop placements and can now accumulate a large quantity of buy orders they know they will later be able to sell when the market takes off into the next phase.

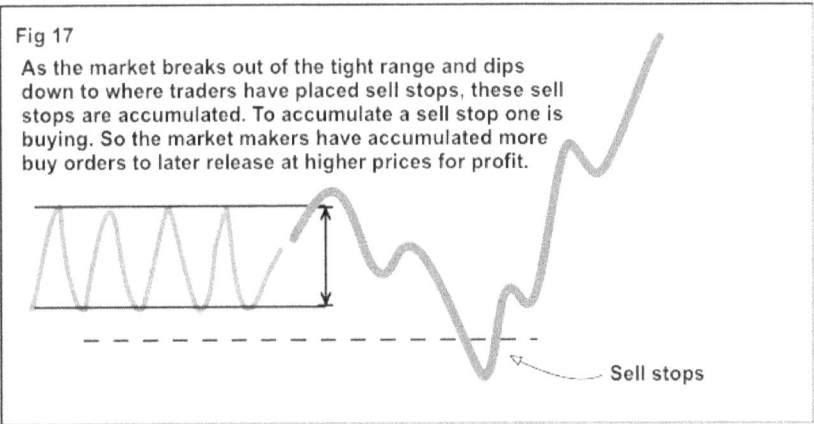

Fig 17

As the market breaks out of the tight range and dips down to where traders have placed sell stops, these sell stops are accumulated. To accumulate a sell stop one is buying. So the market makers have accumulated more buy orders to later release at higher prices for profit.

How this stop run accumulation takes place

For the market makers to accumulate many buy orders very quickly, all they have to do is to drive the market down past where the stop loss orders will be triggered. As these orders are triggered, the market makers buy the sell stops, thus accumulating huge blocks of buy orders at bargain prices (Fig 17).

As these buy orders are accumulated, the market makers hand is just being revealed, and quickly prices will be marked up, taking the market higher.

The market maker, in what is often a very fast move has accumulated large numbers of (in this example BUY orders) at bargain basement prices which lowers the overall average price of all the stock he holds.

This low average price of his stock means that he only needs a small increase in market price to be able to start selling into the rise and thus release his profits.

Manipulation

To fully understand manipulation, it is important to have a full understanding of how beliefs work. To appreciate the interpretation of beliefs offered here, it is important you examine your own beliefs about certain aspects of your life and how they make you and your world what it is at this given moment.

All of us hold beliefs about ourselves, others and everything around us. These beliefs dictate our daily actions to a considerable extent.

Generally speaking, we will only carry out a task which contains an element of risk, if we believe we can manage that risk and survive it.

Imagine there is 6-inch wide plank 50 feet high, spanning two buildings. You need to get from one building to another. As you look down, the possibility of falling will cause you to question your belief you will be able to make it across. The very same plank on the ground will not threaten this belief in your ability to succeed in crossing. It is your belief in the possibility you will fall that creates the conflict.

Another important thing about beliefs is that it is only possible to hold one belief about a particular idea at any one time. In the example of the plank, one cannot believe it is possible to make it across the plank and at the same time believe it is not.

How does this one sided belief relate to the market? To put it simply, one cannot believe the market will go up and at the same time believe it will go down. No trader will buy a market if he believes the price is going to fall and no trader will sell a market he believes is going to rise.

This may seem an obvious observation but for a trader, this has some far reaching implications regarding manipulation and for you as an insider trader.

Up till this point, we only looked at manipulation from the price perspective, and while the price is the ultimate result of manipulation, it is not the price manipulation that causes traders to buy or sell.

Some traders may argue they have no belief about future market direction. While this seems plausible, a belief is inevitably born at some point. When this belief is born, the trader will only take a trade consistent with his belief.

Once the trade has been placed, his belief is suddenly reinforced to the point of all other possible outcomes being rejected. The further the market moves in the anticipated direction, the stronger and stronger the trader's belief will become.

This process may be referred to as "birth of a belief structure." The trader is very vulnerable at this time as irrationality can take over. In many cases indications which show the end of the current market move is ending may be overlooked, leaving the trader in a vulnerable position.

Attachment to a belief structure and reluctance to give it up is completely natural – and is fully exploited by the market makers.

Once you have started mapping the market for manipulated beliefs rather than price, you will be able to understand market activity from the same perspective as the market maker. You will be a knowledgeable and empowered trader.

Price is not the crux of trading. Traders who concentrate on price alone will be unable to observe beliefs and how they are manipulated by the activities of the market makers.

Nothing lasts forever, and belief structures are particularly fickle!

However, for a new belief to be born, a previously held belief must die. This belief death process is always a painful experience because one has to "cut the umbilical cord" to the currently held belief to accept the birth of the new belief. While trading, if you are unable to cut that umbilical cord losses will become inevitable.

The unpleasant experience of taking a loss creates a subconscious association in the trader's mind between changing a belief and pain or stress. This association seriously affects future trading decisions. This subconscious association is what creates the resistance to cutting the umbilical cord. Again another opportunity for the market makers to exploit for their benefit.

Phase Three

Phase three is the profit release phase. This is the phase where the outside traders are actively encouraged to join in and make profits for themselves. However, the only reason this easy profiting is encouraged is because it is during this stage that the outside traders provide the means by which the market makers can release their even greater profits. The market makers must have willing buyers to enter the market so they can sell to these willing buyers. As these buyers enter the market, so the market makers start releasing profits from the buy orders they accumulated during phase one and two.

Let's look at this in graphic format

Now the outsiders can see the market is in up trend they start to buy en-mass. This increased buying adds fuel to the given direction.

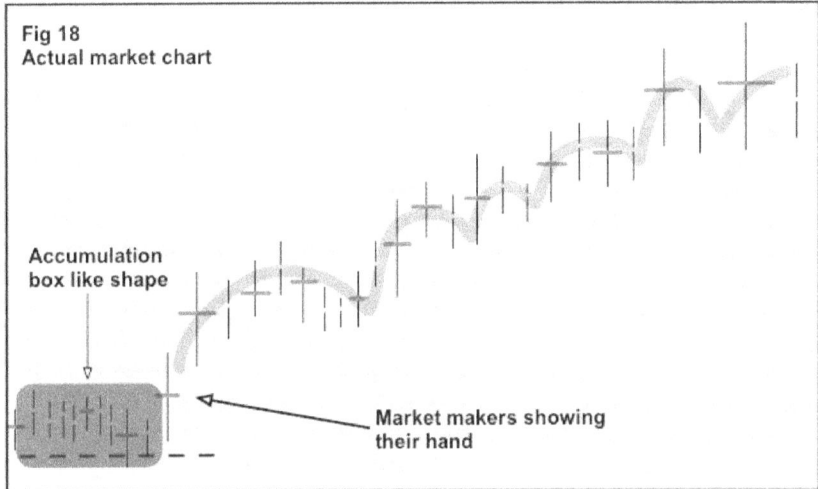

The bars in Fig 18 are actual market bars taken from a real chart. As the market makers show their hand, this creates a flurry of buying activity by outside traders. They are buying from the market makers who had earlier been accumulating buy orders.

For an outside trader to buy, someone must be willing to sell. Who is willing to sell in an 'upward' moving market?

The market maker is pleased to sell to you and actively invites traders (via CLEAR technical analysis signals and news) to join in on the rise. Why?

Because each time a trader buys, the market maker SELLS one of his earlier BUYS to that BUY order at a higher price.

As the market maker is selling to the trader at a price which is higher than his average accumulation price, he is, of course, releasing profits. The higher the market moves, the greater the profit the market maker releases.

PROFIT RELEASE IN A RISING MARKET CYCLE

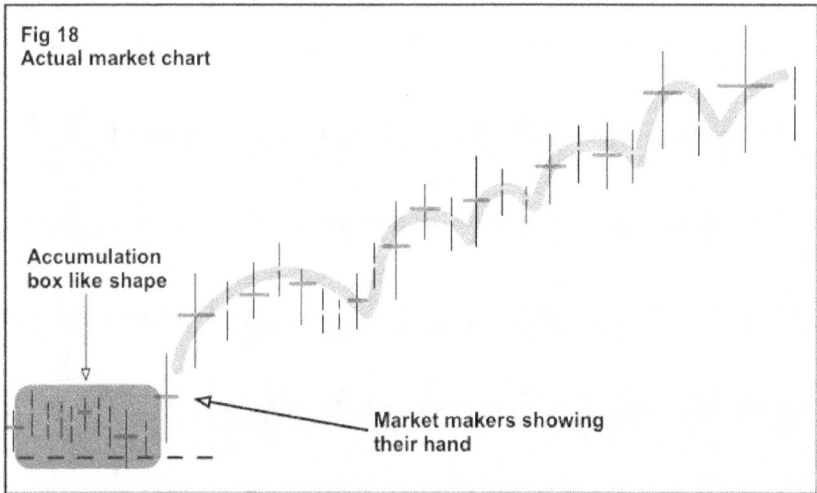

Fig 18
Actual market chart

Accumulation box like shape

Market makers showing their hand

Fig 18 again shows the profit release phase under way, but this time I have marked up each rise and fall on its overall climb.

Once the market breaks from the accumulation area, it might seem like an entirely different scenario starts to play out, that is we just see the market steadily rising over time. Most traders view it exactly this way, and in doing so, they are viewing the FORM the chart is taking and not the CONTENT behind the form.

Let's have a look at this content.

Do you remember this image?

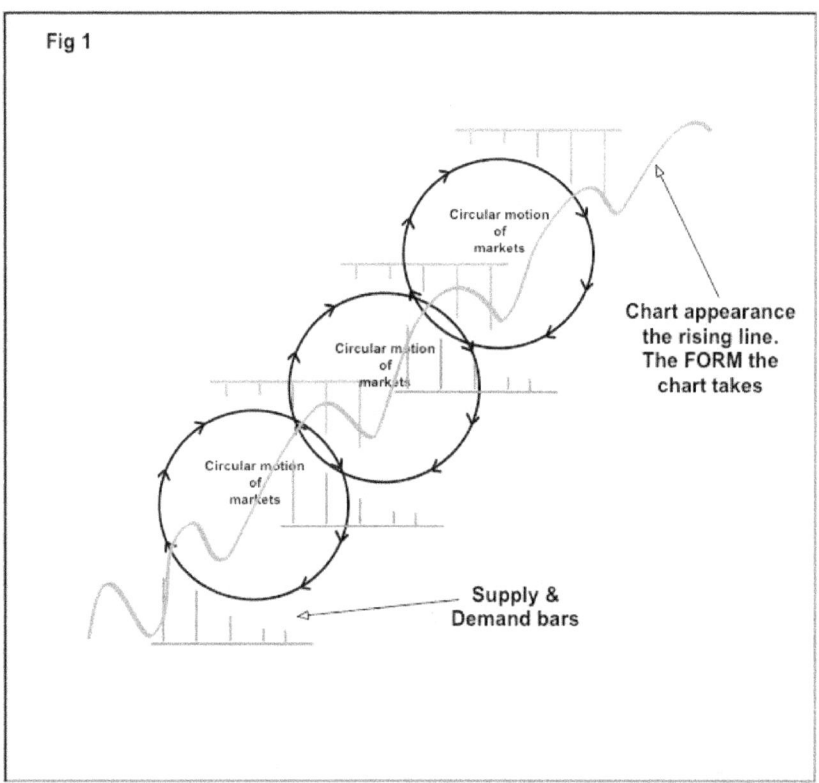

Fig 1

What I would like you to do is mentally superimpose this image Fig 1 over Fig 18(19) repeated below.

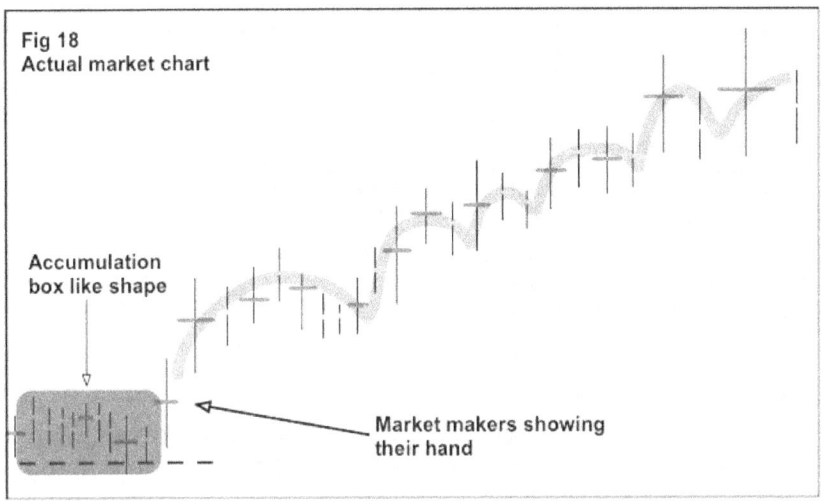

What we can draw from this are some visual similarities, but as mentioned several times before (due to its importance) the visual representation is the form the chart takes over the content. To trade successfully, we must observe form only as a means to read the underlying content. The real and present danger for financial loss is only a momentary mental lapse away from allowing your mind to be drawn into the pattern/form the chart is providing.

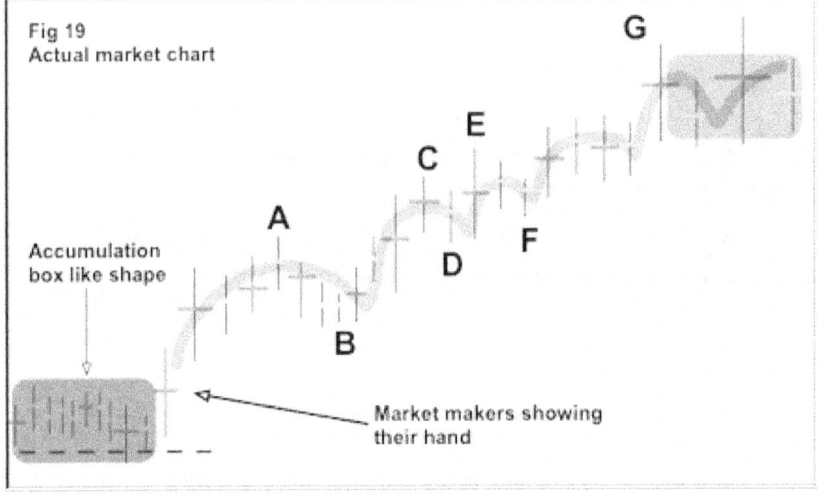

We can see that in Fig 19 once the market makers show their hand, there is a rapid move upwards. This is a deliberate and well calculated move on the part of the market makers. Now they want to be sure outside traders are willing to join in on this upward moving market, which aids their profit release phase.

On fig 19 you will see a rising market up to point (A). It is during the rise that the market maker is rapidly supplying the demand of the outside buyers. He is selling into demand and thus releasing profits from the buy orders he accumulated, at a much lower price.

As this rapid selling or the buy orders into the demand continues, the selling starts to outstrip demand. As a result of this the market will give the appearance of rolling over, of changing direction. It gives the appearance that this moves is running out of steam.

Traders who bought earlier will see this and panic into thinking this was a false move and now the market is likely to go down. They will quickly place stoploss orders and or sell the market, in the anticipation the market is likely to fall from here.

As they sell the market so the market makers will buy the sell orders, thus adding to their original accumulation of buys quota.

When they have absorbed all the selling at (B), the market will quickly rise up to (C), where the process to (D,E,F,G) continues, until the market makers have sold everything they accumulated and then re-accumulated on the way up.

When this process has been completed, the market makers will start the complete process again and return to phase one, the accumulation phase.

It is also during this time the market makers activity causes many popular technical analysis indicators to deliver (in this case) buy signals. However, these signals although correct, will arrive at a time when the trader is extremely vulnerable to a retrace.

Note* During the profit release phase you are actively encouraged to make profits; however, this is only to assist the market maker in making larger profits. When this phase is over, the market maker will then set about taking back the profits he freely encouraged you to take. This is why so many traders report excellent gains to then only see those gains returned to the markets over the following few days.

PROFIT RELEASE IN A FALLING MARKET CYCLE

For the market maker to release profits in a falling market cycle, he must BUY the SELLS he accumulated during his accumulating SELLS cycle. The only way he can do this is if he convinces the outside traders the market is going to fall in value. As you see the form of the market moving down, your mind will lock onto this, and you will want to jump on board. As you enter the market and place a SELL order, the market maker buys back. What has he done? He has just bought from you something he sold earlier at a much higher price. He has released profits!

You will no doubt notice the rise and fall are just a mirror image of each other.

The market makers business model is the same, whether it be a rising or falling market. However, notice that while the FORM of the chart is different, the CONTENT remains the same.

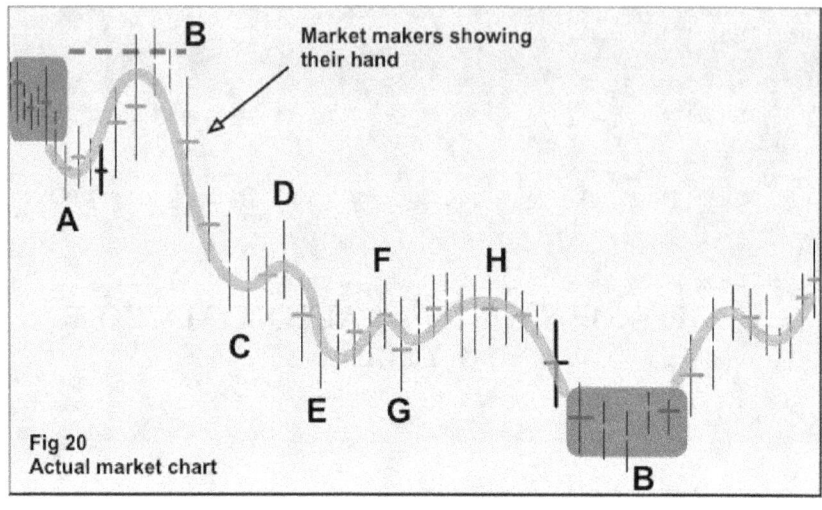

Fig 20
Actual market chart

In Fig 20 we can see (A) the market moves down from the accumulation area but then starts to move up.

Earlier we looked at where traders placed stops. Fig 20 is an example of when a market breaks from the accumulation area. This break gives a good indication of the contents of the accumulation area and encourages outside traders to sell immediately. These traders will place stop loss orders (buy stops) at the top side of the accumulation area. The market makers then manipulate prices to move the market higher, to trigger the buy stops at (B) which they sell to; again they have accumulated more sell orders to fill up their quota.

When they have achieved the desired quota of sell orders, they show their hand to the outside traders, and the price rapidly falls.

The outside traders see the fall and join in by selling. As they sell so, the market maker takes the other side of the sell order which is a buy, but now, of course, his buy allows him to collect profit from the difference in price of that which he accumulated as sells earlier.

*Note. It is imperative at this stage that you fully understand that both the rising and falling market are the same in market makers method. The only difference is whether the earlier accumulation has been buy or sell orders.

MARKET RETRACES

From the preceding Fig 20 can now see that retraces are in fact a truism. We can observe the retraces in our charts. We can justify it in our minds by giving it a name and an associated FORM, and in doing so, we have given meaning to it.

But what's really going on? Why would this happen if the market makers just want to sell into higher and higher prices? Why not just take a market up in a straight line and get it over with?

The reasons are, as always, profit motivated.

Let's now have a look at a retrace from the perspective of a mini cycle of the accumulation phase.

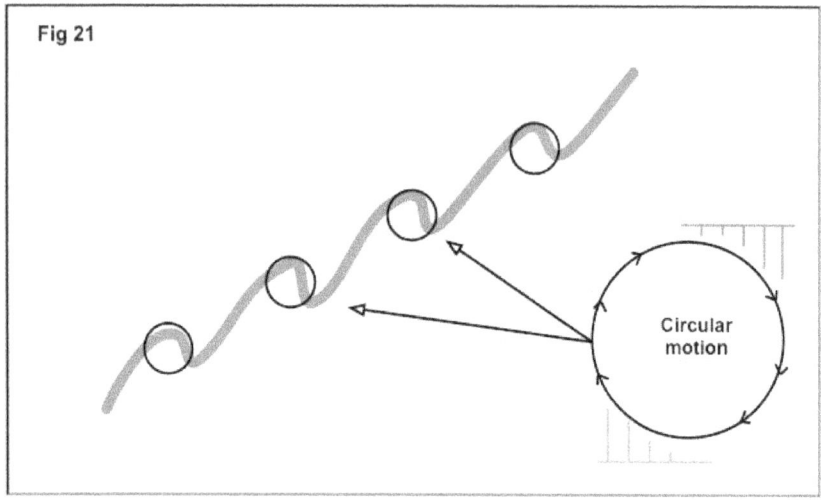

Fig 21

In Fig 21 I have circled small drop backs on the simulated market line. These drop backs in trading terms are referred to as retraces. A retrace is where the price of a stock turns down and retraces into an earlier area that has seen rising prices.

Keep in mind that the same happens in a falling market. Everything is a mirror image.

As a market maker, who has in this example earlier accumulated buy orders, he will know there is good demand and will indeed sell all the buys he earlier accumulated, so why not on the way up to collect some more buys to sell even higher?

As the market starts to rise, those who bought with the market maker are starting to make profits; however, these profits are not bankable cash profits, they are just changing digits on your brokers dealing platform. In order to take possession of profits, the trader will have to close their position by selling what they bought at a lower price.

If the market maker can persuade the trader to close their position and take profits the market maker can buy the sell from the trader. Who is taking those profits?

If this persuasion is successful, the market maker has ACCUMULATED more stock. The stock that he can again sell at a higher price for even more profit for himself later on. Think back to those circle diagrams earlier on.

This now leaves us with a very important question which is:

How can the market maker persuade the outsider trader to sell back to him a perfectly good trading position?

It's called manipulation and this is how it works.

As a trader sees his position move into the money and sees the profits begin to mount, the trader will start to think about not wanting to lose any of those profits. He will need a plan to do this, and that plan is supplied to him via another trading truism.

This truism is called 'locking in profits.'

To lock in profits the trader will move his stop-loss order to protect his paper profits.

Note* Paper profits is the term used for all trades that are open and running.

As the trader moves his stop-loss closer to the live price, so his emotional attachment to the fear of loss will rise and he will become more attached to the trade. This heightened state of awareness produces the effect of closely watching any retrace and forces the trader's mind to focus on the FORM of the chart.

During retraces many traders will close their positions when the market appears to be retracing against their chosen direction. They give birth to the belief that the rise is over.

The next group of traders, who are a little more seasoned, will wait a while to see if this really is a turn or just a retrace. Once this next group sees this was just a retrace, they will now move up their stop-loss orders to the base of what they term as a confirmed retrace, as part of the overall move.

Let's look at this in Fig 22

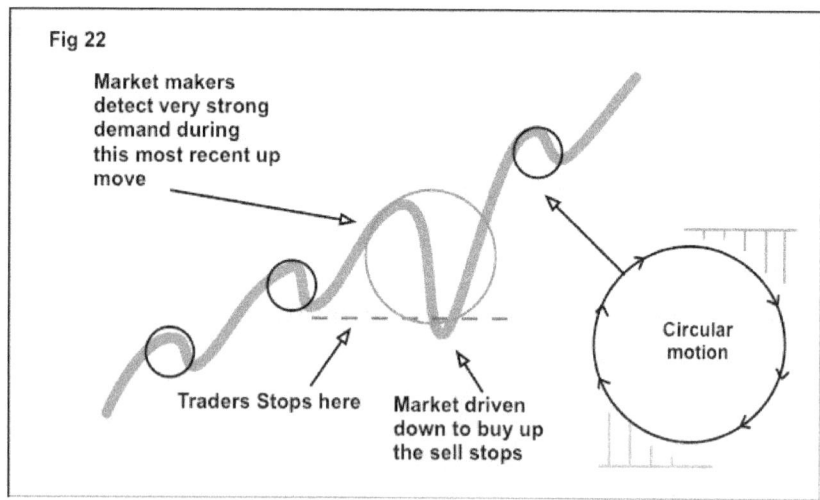

In Fig 22 we see that the more seasoned traders who did not sell their buy orders at the first sign of retrace are more likely to wait for each retrace and then place their stop-loss orders at the base of a retrace. They are following up the lows of each retrace. Seems like a good plan right?

However, if the marker maker detects strong demand on a rise and realises he can sell much more than he accumulated earlier, he will quickly drive the market down below where he knows the more seasoned traders will have placed their stop-loss orders. He will in an instant have achieved more accumulation.

The form the chart takes during this time will also have the effect of causing additional outside traders to sell. The drive down will give birth to a new belief in falling prices.

The market maker, aware of the strong demand, will absorb all the selling by buying and thus accumulating more buy orders. He will then sell these buy orders into the coming ongoing rise. The market makers act of BUYING into the selling also gives support for the market and thus the strength returns and is shown again in the FORM of the chart.

This type of stop take move will generally take place fairly quickly so as to not allow time for the birth of negative beliefs in traders minds about the rise not continuing.

*Note. A stop take is when the price quickly falls or rises (usually validated by some 'unexpected' news that then turned out to not be so bad after all so the stock quickly recovers and continues rising.

It may seem at this stage as if we have departed from the market makers business model and are now covering different traders and their methods but nothing could be farther from the truth. Every aspect of these traders activities are highly predicable and part of the market makers business model. These traders are being guided by the market makers activity into making decisions, which will benefit the market makers.

This is a well ORCHESTRATED MANIPULATION OF TRADERS BELIEFS.

SOME MORE ON STOP LOSS ORDERS

he outside perception of a stop-loss is as the name implies, to stop or limit losses; the inside perception or rather the market makers use of the stop-loss is an accumulation tool.

The predictability of where traders place stops comes about as a result of the truisms traders are given, subtle guidance on 'how to trade' which is freely provided by the many thousands of traders resource portals. One of the most popular questions on these portals is 'where should I place my stop-loss?'

The reason for the popularity of this question is because traders quickly become aware of how often they are stopped out and then see their initial trade later turn into what would have been a big winner for them.

"If only I had held that stock" becomes their mantra, and this happens over and over again.

In Fig 23 you can see how it seems logical and sensible to place stop-loss orders according to rise and falls. You will often hear statements in accordance with this logic that go like:

'That was a support area which will hold.'
   'It's a confirmed retrace price level.'
   'It was oversold at that point, so that is why it went back up.'

These statements sound plausible; they are so plausible that for the most part, they go unchallenged. The truth of the matter is that a retrace area serves the purpose of accumulation by the market makers for their benefit.

Let's break it down visually again.

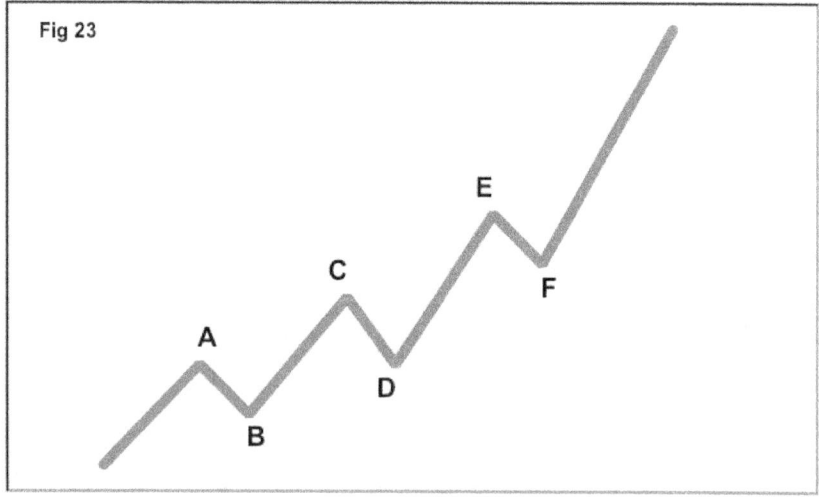

The most popular place for a trader to place a stop-loss order is what is known as (in the case of an upwards moving market) under the most recent reaction.

Fig 23

The traders who are most easily manipulated will start to close their trading positions and take small profits at the first sign of any downturn from point (A) to (B).

Traders who place their stop-loss orders under the retrace to (B) may or may not have their stops targeted, but nevertheless, they are there should the market makers decide to accumulate them.

If the market continues to rise, traders will move their stop-loss orders up, under each subsequent retrace. (B - D - F)

Traders will also place buy orders above where a reaction starts its downturn. (A- C - E)

These traders will place these orders with the logic along the lines of:

If the market goes back above the downturn points (A - C - E) after a retrace, then this will be a good place to buy into the market. This is another widely held trading belief which can place the trader in a very vulnerable position because of where these traders will now place their stop-loss orders. Stop-loss orders that can easily be ACCUMULATED by the market makers should they 'unexpectedly' drive the market down and quickly back up.

Looking back on (A-B-C-D-E-F) note how logical this looks for the trader. So logical and fool proof that some readers may start to think this is a good trading strategy to follow the next time the market moves like this.

This is exactly how most traders are trained, with logical historic charts laid out in this manner. This is trading the FORM the chart is taking, with little or no understanding of the real underlying forces of the CONTENT that we are learning here.

Now what I would like to do is return to the business model of the market maker and examine the FORM of Fig 24. As we do this try to keep in mind the market makers business model.

The example in Fig 24 is representative of the more common chart FORM you will find on an almost daily basis in any market from pork bellies to currencies.

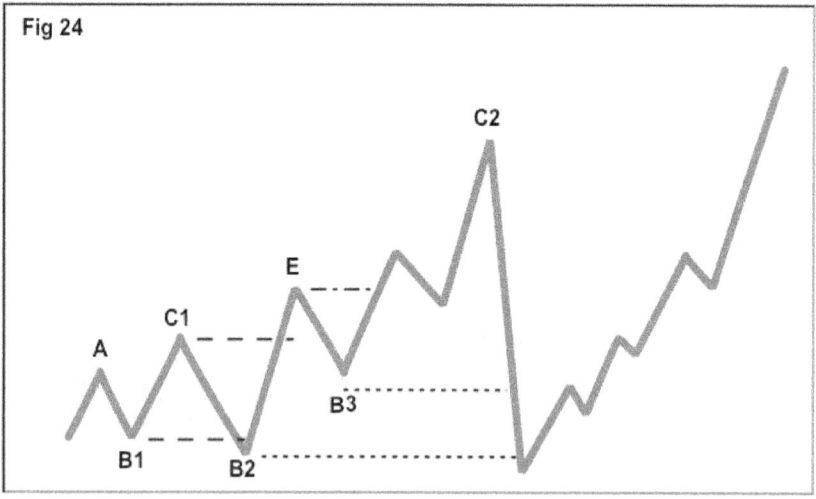

The first thing you will probably notice in Fig 24 is that it is not quite so uninformed; the peaks and dips are not quite so conveniently placed for the trader.

Let's now cycle through this chart from the market makers perspective.

As the market moved up towards, (A) some traders will start to open buy trades; then the market starts its first downturn from (A) to (B1), and some of these traders will close their buy positions and take small profits if possible.

The market makers will buy these sell orders thus accumulating more buys, to later sell at higher prices. This accumulating of buy orders by the market makers will cause the market to rise from (B1) to (C1). Again, on this journey, some traders will open buy orders and will place sell stops at (B1).

As the market then moves up to (C1), the market makers can sell into that rise and thus release profits from the orders (this is not a full profit release phase, rather it is part of the manipulation phase).

By the time the market reaches (C1), outside traders will have placed stop-loss orders at (B1); the marker makers will now start a small downturn by marking the prices down from (C1). Just the same as on the journey from (A) to (B1), some traders will start to sell and take profits, but this time, the market makers will be less willing to absorb these sell orders by buying them. The result will be a faster falling of the market from (C1) to (B2).

As the market moves lower than the low at (B1), the sell stops placed by those traders who bought on the way up from (B1) to (C1) will be triggered. Also at this point, other traders would have set up sell orders under (B1) believing should the market move below (B1), it will continue down.

What happens (in the case of the market makers planning an overall up move) is as the market breaks below (B1), all the sell orders are bought up by the market makers, thus accumulating large numbers of buy orders and causing the market to return to its overall upward trajectory. Again, the market makers are into a profit release up move, as they sell that which they bought at bargain prices at (B2) into the rise on the way up to (E).

Notice the dashed line extending from (C1); here traders will have placed buy orders with the belief that should the market break above (C1) then the market will continue upwards.

The market maker will quickly sell to these buy orders in large quantities, thus causing another drop back towards (B3). Again, a further accumulation of buy orders for the market makers for a later profit release phase.

This process repeats itself on the way to (C2) and on the way, the market starts to show its VISIBLE FORM of an overall upward trend on its way to (C2).

The trend traders are starting to see their technical analysis tools indicating upwards, and confidence levels are building for a continuing rise.

If at this stage the market maker had a strong market and wants to accumulate more buy orders, all that is required is an excuse to rapidly mark down prices to create a fall. As this fall passes lower than the stop-loss orders placed on the way up at (B2-B3), this will trigger the sell stops of the outside traders and allow the market makers to accumulate at bargain basement prices, to later sell into a profit release rise.

As I am writing this, the GBPUSD currency pair has just completed one such cycle. Fig 25-2 shows the actual market chart.

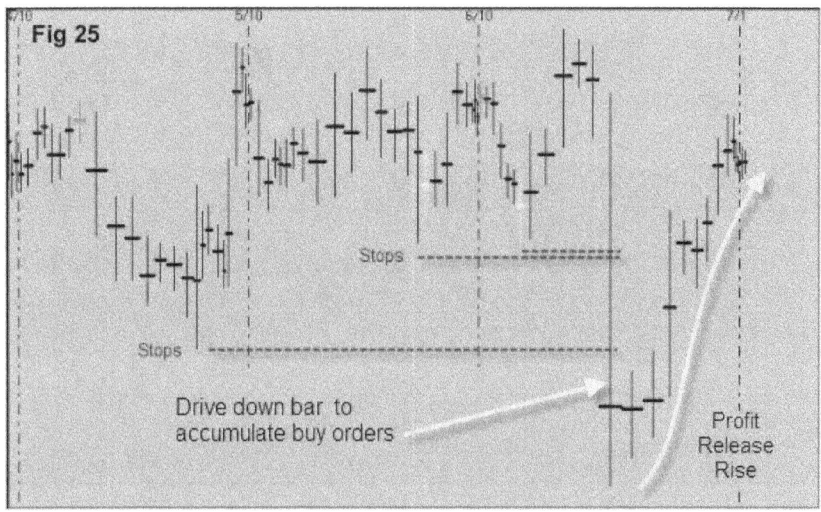

It is to be hoped that you are now starting to realize that much of what is portrayed about the market as being complex is misleading. In reality, markets are far removed from complexity and are rather a highly efficient profit generating machine for the benefit of the few, at a cost to the many.

As I was making some edits to this book (September 2017 - a good six years after original publication), I happen to open up a chart of the GBPNZD Fig 25-2 The chart is a 1-hour time frame - date 12th Sept 2017.Compare Fig 25-2 against Fig 25

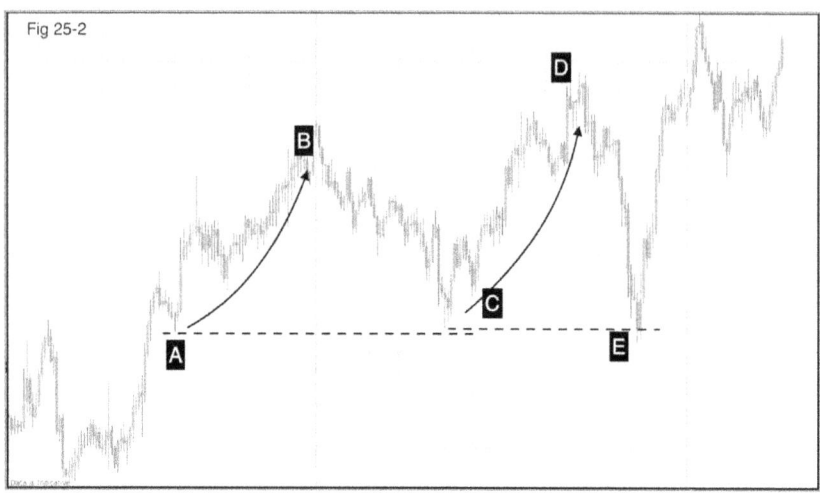

Fig 24 is my drawing to show you a process. Fig 25-2 is the same process but from an actual chart. If you look at the FORM of the Fig 25-2, you may just see the chart shape. However, if you look at the CONTENT you will see:

Traders that bought on the way from (A) to (B) will have placed stop loss orders under (A)

From (B) down to (C) many of these traders will have been given new beliefs that the market had turned, and these traders would close their orders. This move down from (B) to (C) did not collect stops under (A) Why?

Because there were so few there after the move from (B) to (C) caused most traders to close their positions.

Next, the market goes back to the underlying trend of upwards. Traders buy again from (C) to (D) Where do these traders place their stops?

Under the safest low in the house... (A) with the reasoning based on the FORM of the chart that the market had tried to go lower than (A) but it could not so this is a SAFE place for stop loss orders.

From (C) to (D) the market makers KNOW there is underlying strength in the market. They sell all their accumulated stock into this rise from (C) to (D), so they need more stock - more BUYS.

They drive the market down from (D) and so set up beliefs that the uptrend is over which encourages the masses to SELL. They BUY the SELLS to accumulate BUYS.

(Notice how fast the prices fall from (D) to (E) relative to how they rose from (C) to (D)

They drive the market just below (C) and then (A) to pick up the last of the stops and then the market RAPIDLY moves back up to take them instantly above their AVERAGE buy price. Everything now sold into the rise from (E) is pure profit release.

The market makers business model is simple; however, to trade the model requires understanding every step of the way. It requires dedicated practice and ongoing correction until the necessary trading skills become second nature to you.

At some point in this book, you will have a paradigm shift, and you will, from that moment on, view the markets from the inside out, instead of the outside traders, who view it from the outside in. This will be your defining moment as a trader, and for some who may have been trading for many years without success, it can be an emotionally charged experience.

EXITING THE MARKET

I have a trading saying I believe to be true:

> "Any fool can get into a market, but it takes skill to know when to get out."

Today it is so easy to enter any market with a trading position. With a click of your mouse you are in the market live trading, but then what?

To make money from a trading position, that position will have to be closed. If you buy, you will have to sell and if you sell you will have to buy.

    Deciding to close your trade too early or too late is critical to your profitability and therefore critical to your overall success.

Most traders who are not trading the market makers business model can only really use technical analysis tools, such as stop-loss orders, or trailing stops, etc. The problem with this is that you will always be at a disadvantage.

If we take the example of the trailing stop, our minds will logically assume that this method will bring us the best gains. For example, the trader opens a buy position and sees that trade start to move into the money, as the market climbs. We will assume the trader places a 30 pips trailing stop.

The trailing stop means that as the market moves up, so the stop loss order follows, always at a 30 pips distance. When the market starts to move down, the stop-loss stays at its last position, meaning the lower the market falls, the closer your stop-loss order becomes to the current market price. So, if the market retraces back 30 pips, the trader will be stopped out.

Let's look at this in Fig 26

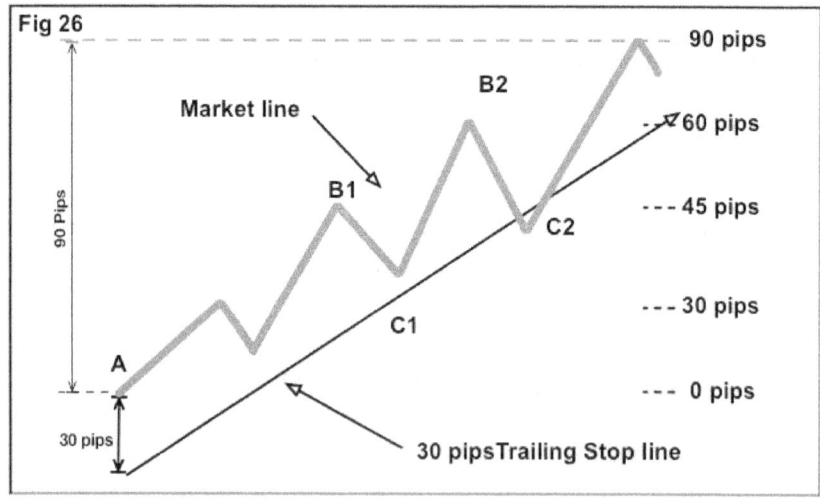

For ease of explanation we will keep the prices to a unit of $1.00, so in this example, we are assuming the trader buys at point (A) a $1.00 lot. At the same time, he places a trailing sell stop-loss order 30 pips

Note* We are keeping this simple and just using the term 'pips' which is a currency trading term to show price scaling.

If the market immediately moved down from (A), this position would be stopped out, and the trader would lose $30.00.

Assuming our trader has opened a trade in the right direction and the market now starts to move upward, he will start to see the trade move into profit.

By the time the trade reaches (B1), the trade will be 45 pips ($45.00) in the money, and the trailing stop-loss will have automatically moved up to 30 pips below (B1). Now if the market retraced 30 pips, our trader would be stopped out and have made 15 pips ($15.00)

In our case, however, we can see our trader was not stopped out, and the market continued up to (B2), so now the trade is 60 pips in the money ($60.00) but now the market retraces down to C2 and crosses the 30 pips trailing stop-loss line and stops out the trader. The trader has made 45 pips ($45.00). We then see the market move on up to touch the 90 pips line, where our traders could have taken 90 pips profit instead of 45 pips. A 100% increase as a result of not using a trailing stop-loss.

Knowing when to get out and take maximum profits is vitally important for the long term success of a trader.

The common belief that a trailing stop-loss allows you to maximise your gains by letting them run is another of our trading truisms. It's a great tool for the market maker to use as an accumulation tool, at the expense of the trader.

Next, the market retraces down past the level of (B1) to (C2) and in doing so, stops the trader out for a $30.00 gain.

This all seems very good; however, note at one point the trader was in the money for $60.00. Further more, had the market not have stopped the trader out at the (B1) level and had continued to the 90 pips peak, the trader would have been in the money to the tune of 90 pips ($90.00) and had a stop-loss back at 60pips profit.

What we can draw from this is that the theory of trailing stops provides open ended gains while minimizing losses, is not correct and a far better description is that trailing stops are an easy way for the market maker to accumulate if that is going to be profitable for him.

Last night while writing this chapter, I was also looking at live markets as they were being traded and saw a trading opportunity present itself.
    In Fig 27 we can observe how that trade would have turned out if I had used a trailing stop-loss.

Exiting the market

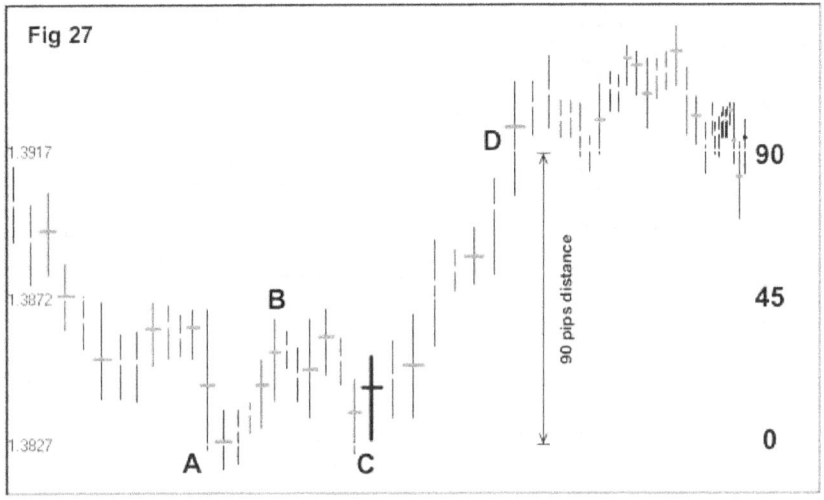

I bought the at (A) at a market price of 1.3827 and placed a 25 pips stop-loss at 1.3802. It was very late here in New Zealand when I opened this trade, so I had to go to bed almost immediately the trade was opened, but as we can see later on the market moved up to (B) 1.3870, and my trading position was then 43pips in the money. If I had used a trailing stop, my stop-loss would now be 30 pips below at 1.3840.

This would now mean that as the market retraced down to (C) I would have been stopped out at 1.3840 and made a profit of 13 pips.

What happened was that I achieved a profit of 90 pips because I had planned where to close this trade BEFORE I opened it.

Now let's take a look at when to close trades.

As a trader, one thing you will quickly be faced with is the question, where do you exit your trades?

In this example, I exited at a predetermined level of 90 pips higher than where I entered, but just applying a numerical target like this, whilst highly accurate is not a trading solution in itself. You must understand WHY to close a trade.

To answer the WHY question, we have to return to the market makers business model, we have to look at this from his perspective.

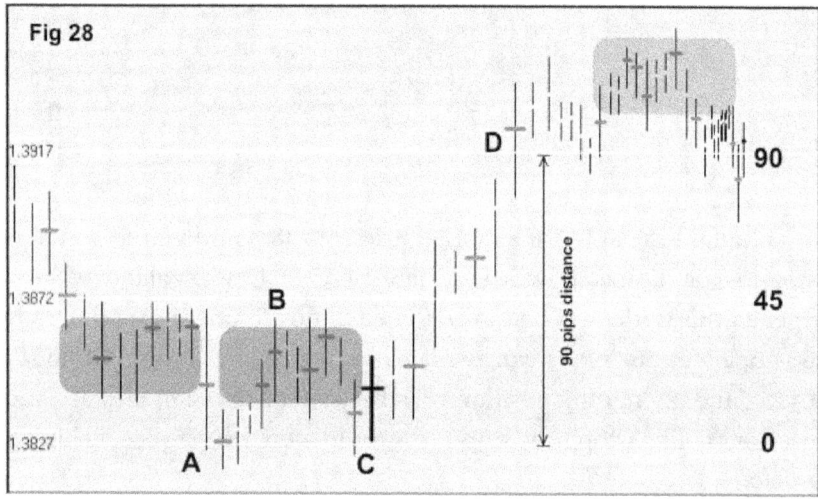

In Fig 28 we can see in the lower shaded areas, there was accumulation going on. As the market moved down to (A), the market makers also accumulated further orders (off the screen to the left was a level where traders had placed sell stops, which the market makers bought thus accumulating buy orders).

It was the outcome of this stop taking which revealed the market makers contents of the box; it revealed they had previously been accumulating buy orders.

As we know from an earlier explanation, the only way for the market maker to make money from an accumulation of buy orders is for the market to rise. However, how far will the market rise?

To answer this question, we can use a fundamental rule of doing business which the market maker is forced to comply with:

You cannot sell what you do not have, and even if you could, you could not release any profit from this activity.

This means that any move the market maker instigates will end when all he accumulated has been released for profit. No further movement will take place until the market maker has again run his accumulation phase.

This simple rule of doing business provides us with the very best exit levels, at which point we can take our profits.

Let's now turn things on their head in Fig 29

106   Exiting the market

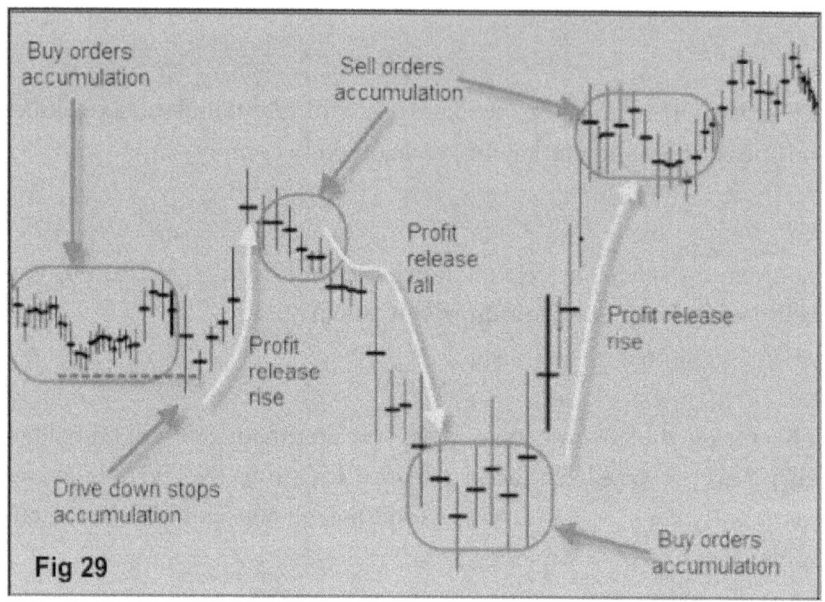

Fig 29

What you should be able to draw from Fig 29 is that entry and exit are intertwined. It has to be this way because the market markets business model is a never ending cycle of accumulation, manipulation and profit release.

However, to provide a more consistent way of exiting for the best return possible, the trader of the market makers business model should be aware of the consistency of the profit release phase to cover a distance of around 90 pips. Whilst this consistency is difficult to convey in a written format, you will soon discover this consistency for yourself from your own market charts. I urge you to open up some charts and start looking for 90 pip ranges. For ease of starting out do this using currency pairs.

Now its time to get back to the driving force behind all price movement.

4
THE POWER OF BELIEF

Everything you are today, right down to this very moment, can be reduced down to the beliefs we hold about ourselves Our next thought will be based upon our currently held beliefs. Freewill? Only so far as our beliefs allow.

Beliefs affect the market

We can say with certainty that you as a trader, will not buy something you believe will fall in price and reward you with a loss. Likewise, you will not sell something you believe will rise in price rewarding you with a loss.

YOU CANNOT and will not act until you have developed (given birth to) a belief about the future. If you doubt that statement - try it.

HOWEVER, apart from the individual trader's belief, there are also group beliefs and commitment to those beliefs. This commitment is a very important part of trading.

I FOUND A WIDELY HELD definition of the word commitment which suits us well. That definition was:

 "An obligation that may be mutual or self-imposed."

Let's first deal with the mutual obligation. A mutual obligation can be defined for the trader, when we see other traders taking actions, we feel obligated to take.

TO BETTER UNDERSTAND THIS, it may help to create an image in your mind. Imagine you're standing high up on a cliff overlooking the ocean. Floating on the ocean, you can see thousands of hand folded little paper boats. As you observe these boats, you notice that every time there is a slight breeze, so the boats jostle and then start to drift in the direction of the breeze. As this breeze starts and stops from different directions, create the image in your mind how those little boats would react.

NEXT, further imagine that within each boat is the mind of a trader. This mind is trying to work out, or better put trying to predict, the next direction the boats will move in. There is, however, one problem, which is that the mind of the trader cannot feel the breeze and can only predict the next direction, based on the action or reaction of the other boats.

THIS IMAGINARY SCENE represents how I view the market. Traders are developing beliefs about future price, based upon what they believe to be the reactions of other traders. These reactions, however, are all interrelated; they are all connected and created by the effects of a breeze, and the breeze is being created by the market makers. You are looking at the FORM of the market on a chart and being influenced by that form. What we can draw from this is that a trader's mind is in reality, highly dependent upon the minds of other traders - or at this stage better put, the beliefs those traders' minds hold, beliefs which may or may not be true.

From the point of view of sitting in one of those boats, we can now see that it would be near impossible to predict, with any degree of certainty, the beliefs in the minds in other boats. What we need to do is to climb out of the boat and navigate our way back to the top of the hill. On the top of this hill, we will find the market makers perspective.

We need to view the market from the same perspective as the market makers. We need to look at all the little boats, not from the perspective of the shape or pattern they make sitting on the water, but rather by the contents which are being mass manipulated.

BELIEFS MOVING MARKETS

Once we understand how beliefs work and what the commitment to those beliefs will translate into, we can start to understand more clearly how market makers move a market. The outside perception is markets are price driven, but this is not true because at the back of every buy or sell is a traders belief that this trade will be a winning trade. It is only when the trader develops this belief that he will be able to push the button to either buy or sell, in alignment with his belief.

But of course, beliefs can and do change.

CHANGING BELIEFS

Beliefs change in one of two ways; a sudden reception of something we instantly know to be true or slowly over time.

As an example of a sudden shift in belief, we could use the example of the first report of a flying machine. Previously to that historic event, it was widely believed a man would never fly. Newspapers and very early television destroyed that belief forever when the forever famous brothers took to the air.

In that instant, everyone who saw this experienced an instant belief shift to some degree. There would have of course been others who did not see the flight, did not read the newspapers and would only have heard the news second hand from other sources. This group, faced with an existing firmly held belief man would never fly, would gradually over time, be forced to give up their old belief and accept the new one.

At this point, I think it safe to say and hard to deny that it is a traders belief in the future price of a stock which allows a trading decision to either buy, sell or do nothing.

Following this train of reasoning forward to the larger market, I think it is also safe to say and hard to deny that markets are not price driven, but are in fact driven by beliefs traders hold about where the price will move to in the future.

Herein lies the premise:

> MARKET MAKERS DO NOT MANIPULATE PRICE, THEY MANIPULATE BELIEF!

Let's now have a look at how market information is presented to the trader and what effect this has.

CHARTING THE MARKETS

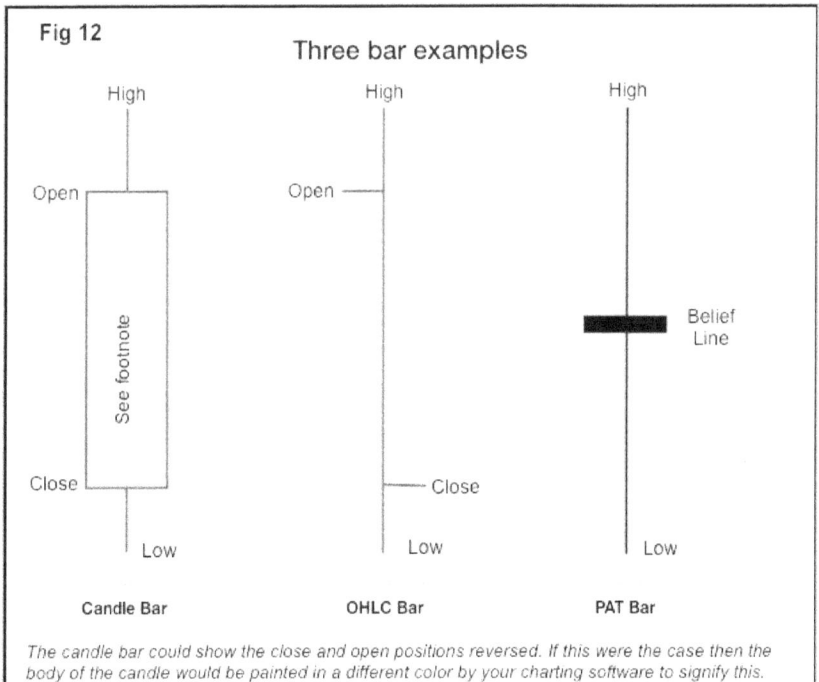

Fig 12 — Three bar examples

The candle bar could show the close and open positions reversed. If this were the case then the body of the candle would be painted in a different color by your charting software to signify this.

Fig 12 depicts a Candle bar, an Open - High - Low - Close bar and a PAT bar. Let's compare the three examples from left to right and see what they are displaying to us.

From the left, we have the candle bar. When this bar closed at the end of its respective time period, it displays to us:

1. Where the market price was at the beginning of the time frame (Open)
2. The highest price the market traveled to during the time frame (High)
3. The lowest price the market traveled to during the time frame (Low)
4. Where the market price was at the end of the time frame (Close)

Note* Time period is the time it takes for the bar to open and close. This can be any setting on your trading software from 1 min to yearly.

In the OHLC bar, we can see the same information is provided to us minus the aesthetic body of the candle.

On the far right is the PAT bar. The first thing you may notice about this bar is that it does not contain any information regarding the opening and closing price.

The PAT bar consists of only two elements. The first being the vertical line, similar to all other charts shows the high and low prices traded to in the respective time frame being charted. The second element is the horizontal line the crosses the vertical line. This is known as the belief bar or belief line.

The belief line represents our collection of little paper boats, each with a trader sitting inside.

Note* PAT is the abbreviated name of my personal trading software. This software is very briefly covered at the end of the book. This software is not required to trade the market makers method. This is my personal choice as a trading TOOL, there are many tools on the market, and you need to use one that you are comfortable with.

The message of the belief line (bar)

The belief line is a representation of the collective beliefs of traders relative to the highest and lowest prices trading in the respective time frame.

Given that we know a trader will not buy or sell anything until a belief develops this belief line can give us insight into what is happening in the market.

I believe it fair to say the position of the belief line, relative to other belief lines, offers us real insight into predicting future market direction.

Earlier, I discussed the idea of changing beliefs over time or having beliefs changed in an instant. I would now like to further explain this idea with the use of some graphics and an imaginative story called 'climbing stairs in the dark.'

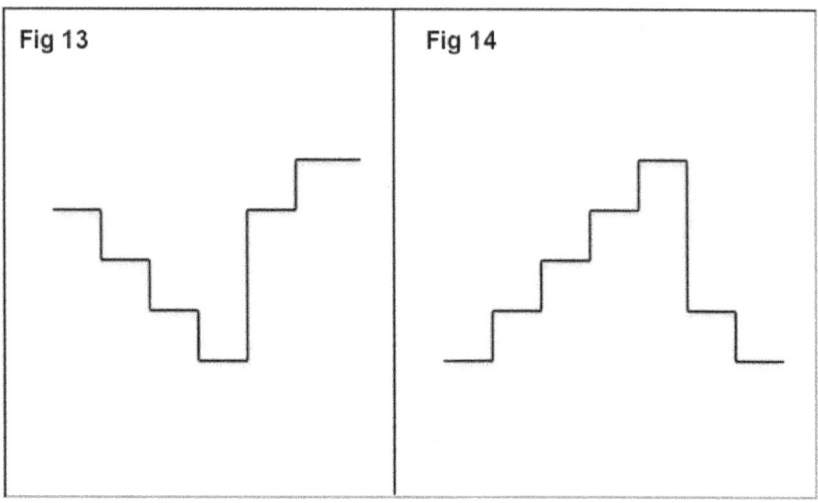

Imagine you are in a dark room unable to see anything at all. As you stumble around, you discover some steps, Fig 13. You start to descend in complete darkness, lower and lower you go gaining increasing confidence and developing a belief that the next step is like the preceding one, going to be a down step.

Then all of a sudden there is no down step, and a big jump up step confronts you.

Now you move to another room Fig 14.

Again, you find some steps, and you climb higher and higher as you build confidence in the next step being up. Then suddenly, the next step is down, and it provides and unpleasant jar to your body.

What would your state of mind be like now if you had to enter the third room and start with the third set of steps? Try to physically experience the effect this would have on you.

The reason I want you to try to physically experience this story is because I want you to understand these feelings and how they manifest in your fellow trader. When you understand your fellow trader, and you realize they will react like you, then you will be able to understand market movement on a much deeper level. You will be able to understand market movement in a way that gives you the confidence to trade any market.

Now we will take the steps story and apply it to the market.

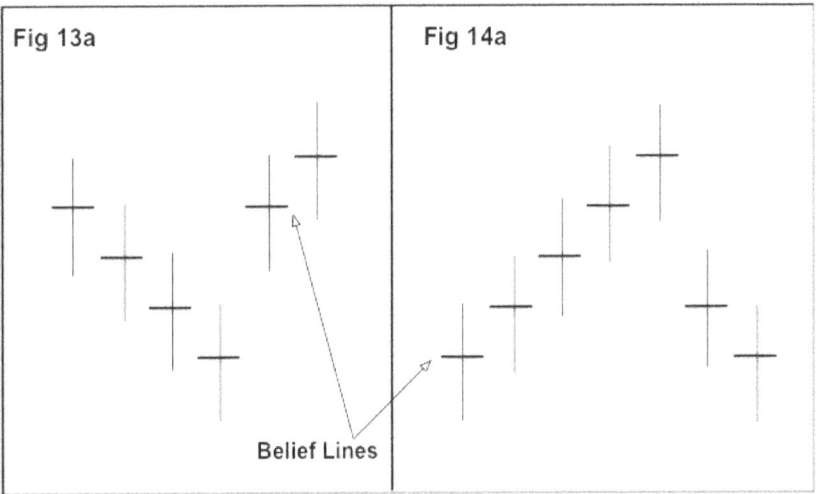

Figs 13a and 14a are the same as Figs 13 and 14 with the exception that vertical line of the imaginary steps are grayed out, and an added vertical price line is running through the center of each belief line. Figs 13a and 14a now represent what a PAT bar chart would look like.

The belief lines in this chart, enable you to view sudden shifts in traders beliefs regarding price. Reading this information backward to an accumulation area can often provide supporting evidence as to whether the market makers are accumulating buy or sell orders. Remember, once you know which side of the market, buys or sells are being accumulated you are by default placed into a very powerful position for financial gain.

5

UNDERSTANDING MARKET BELIEFS

The revelation of the astonishing degree of consistency in beliefs came to me during live trading courses I conducted many years ago. To test the belief threshold of a group of students, I devised a simple exercise.

I WOULD GIVE each student an A4 sheet of graph paper. I then explained that I was going to flip a coin. Each time heads came up, the students marked an X one box higher and for tails, one box lower.

The exercise started with one X being placed in the center, on the left-hand side of the paper.

EACH STUDENT MARKED the results of my coin flipping on graph paper. What we were doing was simulating the FORM of a market chart. The number of flips was plotted on the X axis, while the Y axis, starting from a center line, indicated whether a tail or a head had come up.

I ASKED the students to observe if any FORM appeared as a result of the coin tossing.

They were to question if the form might indicate when we got to the end of the paper, the plot, might finish above or below the center point.

I ALSO ASKED for them to mark an important the point on their imagined market chart. This point would indicate where they developed a belief that by the time they got to the end of the paper, the finish point would be, above or below the mid line.

They were also asked to sign their name at this point.

NOTE* The act of signing something is an important recorded commitment.

FURTHER INSTRUCTIONS WERE if the 'simulated market' caused them to change their mind they were to mark the point where they changed their mind and to again, sign their name.

I THEN STARTED to misrepresented the results of the coin tossing, so the plot was well above the starting point after a small number of throws. Once I observed the participants had committed themselves to the belief that the "simulated market" would finish above the starting point, I began to manipulate the results in the opposite direction.

This seemingly innocuous exercise revealed some fascinating phenomena.

THE ALTERNATION from comfort to discomfort, when the plot moved against them and then relief when a few calls brought it back was observable. The astonishing thing was that although the students were unable to see each other's charts, they were all similar concerning the points at which their beliefs had developed, and they signed their name.

I THEN TOOK the results and overlaid them onto actual market charts. This revealed that I could predict with a high degree of accuracy, where a trader was likely to develop beliefs about future direction.

I COULD ALSO OBSERVE consistencies where the trader would change their mind about their initial trade. No matter what market I overlaid this on, the results were consistent.

THE OUTCOME of this exercise made it clear to me that the way in which traders' beliefs are given birth to and how they change over time, could be used in formulating an efficient trading method.

LET'S look a little deeper into this.

USING BELIEFS IN A DECISION MAKING PROCESS

Imagine waiting at curbside to cross a busy road. There is one lane coming at you from the right, a central reservation and beyond that, a lane coming from the left.

How are you going to cross this road?

Most will say, 'Wait until the road is clear and then cross.' This, of course, is the logical answer. It 'seems' like this is all one requires to cross the road. However, it runs a lot deeper than this.

You will not be able to step off the curb until a belief is born within you that says you can make it to the other side or at least to the central reservation. Without this belief, you will be rooted to the spot. You will need to give birth to this belief before you can step out into the road.

Now imagine another curb side instance on the same road, but now there are others standing beside you, also wanting to cross. They, like you, are looking for a gap in the traffic. Suddenly, one of them steps out, and you join them, and in that instant, you realize this was not the best idea.

Chances are you would have at one time or another; perhaps many times experienced these two events. The difference between these two events is your key to understanding what a manipulated belief feels like.

In the first instance, you created your belief. You gave birth to this belief.
 In the second instance, someone else's belief caused you to step off the curb.

The subtle difference between these two beliefs and how you can detect that difference is vitally important to understand, from a trading perspective.

Market makers will always be stepping off the curb, creating beliefs in outside traders that now is the time to cross the road, now is the time to join the market.

Market makers are in the belief creation business. They want to get you to enter the market when they want you to; you will have to generate a belief saying you are going to win this next trade. It's only at this point you will then enter the market in the direction you believe will be profitable, either up or down.

However, is this your belief? Or has this belief been forced upon you like the person stepping out beside you to cross the road?

When you can ACTIVELY decipher where your trading belief came from you will have made a huge leap towards successful trading.

Let's have a look at this in chart format.

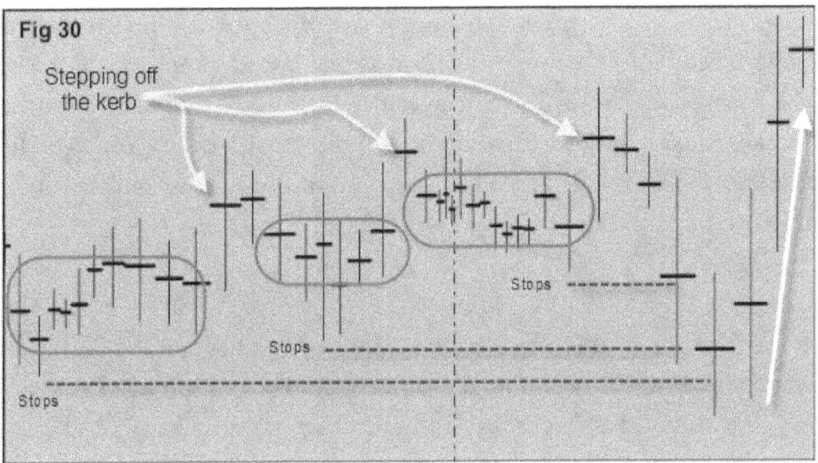

In fig 30, you see three boxed areas. We have discussed these before with the label accumulation areas, a description that still stands. However, I would like you to consider these accumulation areas as groups of people building up on the curb line, waiting to cross the road.

The three arrows point to a dramatic shift, the market makers have stepped off the curb to cross the road, to encourage others, to follow. All the traders left sitting on the curb be likely saying to themselves "is it safe to cross the road?" Some traders will follow, only to find almost immediately it was not safe.

The traders who had their beliefs manipulated into crossing the road will now place stop loss orders according to trading truisms, at a previous low.

Later, we will see the same process repeated and each time traders are manipulated into the market and manipulated into where they place their stop loss orders.

These traders, over time, will start to see their poor trading positions move a little into the money then, after the last 'stepping off the curb,' the market is driven down triggering all the sell orders which the market makers buy up, thus adding to their stock of buy orders. The market then reverses and heads up, where the market makers enter into their profit release phase.

It is important at this stage that you start to look beyond the FORM of the chart. The chart is only a graphical representation of prices and looking at it in this way, offers little insight to the trader.

By looking THROUGH the chart, by looking at how traders beliefs are manipulated and then overlaying that information onto the market makers business model - Accumulation, manipulation, and profit release, you are able to get an unprecedented look into the real workings of the market.

Hopefully, by now you are starting to realize that the shape of a bar, a moving average, a pattern formation, far from providing you with information, is clouding the real information which will allow you to profit.

Trading decisions should never be made in the heat of the moment; you should not take a trade just because someone else jumps out in the road. All trading decisions should always be part of the overall market makers business model and also by asking yourself what is the market makers execution strategy this time?

THE MARKET MAKERS STRATEGY (METHOD)

By the way, did you know you DON"T need to develop a trading strategy?

Whenever I speak the above sentence to a group of traders, it is frequently followed by a lengthy silence, some disbelief and then, often a little-vented frustration.

Thinking about it, the reaction is reasonable; after all, many of these traders have been devising trading strategies for years. Many of them have become experts in all forms of technical analysis, and they love strategies. Suddenly, they are faced with cutting what is perceived to be the umbilical cord that is keeping their strategies alive, and they don't like it.

To calm things down, I quickly say I will give them all a strategy they can observe with clarity, they can endlessly analyze for validity and then they can use for profit.

Suddenly everyone is happy again; however, I then say that before I give them this strategy, we should first understand the market makers strategy. After all, there are only three, so we may as well learn them. Everyone agrees.

The market makers business model is:

1. Accumulation
2. Manipulation
3. Profit release

These three points are their business model, this is how they make money. The model is in many ways no different to opening a shop, and just like the shop that needs customers to make the business model function, so too the market maker need customers. People need to be persuaded to enter the shop and traders need to be persuaded to enter the market.

For the market makers accumulation phase to be successful, they need a strategy. This strategy must allow them to accumulate either buy or sell orders (depending upon the ultimate direction of the market) without alerting the outside traders. The method for this is to keep the market trading in a tight range. This range is NOT congestion. (Truism) This is a very active time of ACCUMULATION.

Keeping the markets in a tight range, restricts the birth of beliefs in traders' minds about any one particular direction, it creates an environment where the market makers can covertly accumulate the side of the market they desire.

However, the longer this tight range continues, there will also be a decreasing number of traders who will enter the market. This is quite normal as interest starts to fall away.

Most traders who are trading using traditional trading indicators, will try to associate this falling interest to one side of the market, either buying or selling. Not only is this impossible to know for sure, this type of thinking and analysis will start to build beliefs about which way you think the market is likely to move from here. The very moment you create such a belief, you will become committed to that side of the market, even in the face of contrary market activity.

At this stage then, we can state that there are two market makers strategies for the accumulation phase. These two strategies involve a tight trading range and stop taking. With very little practice you should have little difficulty in spotting both of these strategies being used.

You might like to break here and go and look for this one your chart. However, be on your guard that your mind does not just say 'ok here is the pattern' because that would be looking at FORM. Keep in mind what you are really observing.

Just before we leave the stop taking accumulation strategy, can you work out how this can be used to predict future market direction?

If the market makers drive a market down to take out sell stops, they will be buying those sell stops. If the market makers are accumulating buy orders, then their intention can only be to drive the market higher and sell those buy orders at a higher price later on.

You might want to read the above paragraph one more time....It's giving you something rather powerful.

Just before we move onto the second part of the market makers business model, that being manipulation, maybe now is a good time to ask a question.

Which is...

Do you need to devise a personal trading strategy if the market makers BUSINESS MODEL is as consistent as the rising sun and it provides you with a method to continually profit?

THE MARKET MAKERS MANIPULATION STRATEGY

The market makers manipulation strategy, unlike the accumulation strategy, is not covert at all, if it were covert, it would have no effect and thus not provide the market maker with any benefit.

Do you remember the paper boat analogy? This is where we get to examine this in more detail.

We will for this example, assume the market maker has completed part one of his accumulation strategy, the covert accumulation of (in this example) buy orders.

As explained earlier, it will nearly always be impossible to accumulate the full desired quota in this manner, due to what will be increasing apathy as the market range decreases, along with the volume of activity.

The manipulation strategy of the market makers will be to manipulate the beliefs of the outside traders so that they will place orders in the wrong direction. The preferred and most consistent method of achieving this is by moving the price steadily in a direction towards a high or low price, very close to the current market activity. Let's have a look at this in chart form.

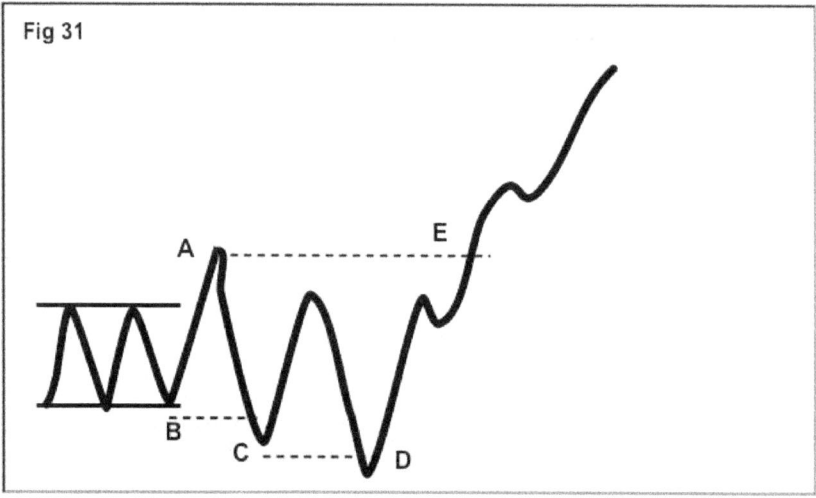

Fig 31

Here in Fig 31, we can see the market makers have completed their first strategy of accumulation, shown by the box. (we are assuming accumulation of buy orders in this instance).

During this time, outside traders would have also have purchased buy orders, because while they do not know the market makers are accumulating buys, they believe the market is likely to go up.

Important to keep in mind that these traders' beliefs will be reinforced by any upward movement. The reinforcement of beliefs is a powerful effect on the trader.

By the time the market reaches the point (A), the outside traders who bought within the market makers accumulation area will now be feeling good about their trading decisions. They are likely to place their sell stops (with the idea of preventing losses) at the underside of the box like accumulation area (B).

If the market continued up from (A), the market makers would not have the opportunity to accumulate more buy orders, and thus their profit release phase will be dramatically reduced.

The market makers at point (A) are likely to sell a block of orders that will have the effect of turning the market down towards (C). This turning down will provide them with the opportunity to pick up many buy orders as traders start to sell

Do you remember the traders who bought earlier on and placed their sell stop loss orders at (B)?

Now as the market turns down to (C), the sell stops will be triggered at (B), and the other side of a sell order is a buy. Thus the market makers accumulate the sell stops as buy and the market rises.

Traders see this and also start to buy, they will place their sell stops at (C).

At this stage, if the market maker has accumulated all the buy orders he knows he can sell into the demand then the market would continue directly up from (C) and beyond (D) into the profit release phase.

If the market maker wants to accumulate more buy orders, then he will repeat the process of taking the market below (C) to (D), again triggering the sell orders which he accumulates as buy orders.

This type of market activity is manipulation. The market makers are manipulating the market, but ultimately they are shaping the beliefs traders hold about future market direction. Once the market maker has accumulated all the buy orders he desires, he will move to phase three and strategy three.

THE PROFIT RELEASE STRATEGY

The profit release strategy is the easiest to orchestrate. It will be kicked off by either or a mixture of:

A rapid price move out of the final accumulation area
    A news release
    A rapid movement in another market.

In short, anything that can justify a rapid mark up of prices.

This phase has some very clear characteristics, the reason they are clear is that this is where the OUTSIDE TRADER ARE ACTIVELY INVITED AND ENCOURAGED TO MAKE MONEY.

Without the willing participation of the outside traders at this point, the market makers will be left holding the bag with nowhere to go.

But now, where will the market move to?

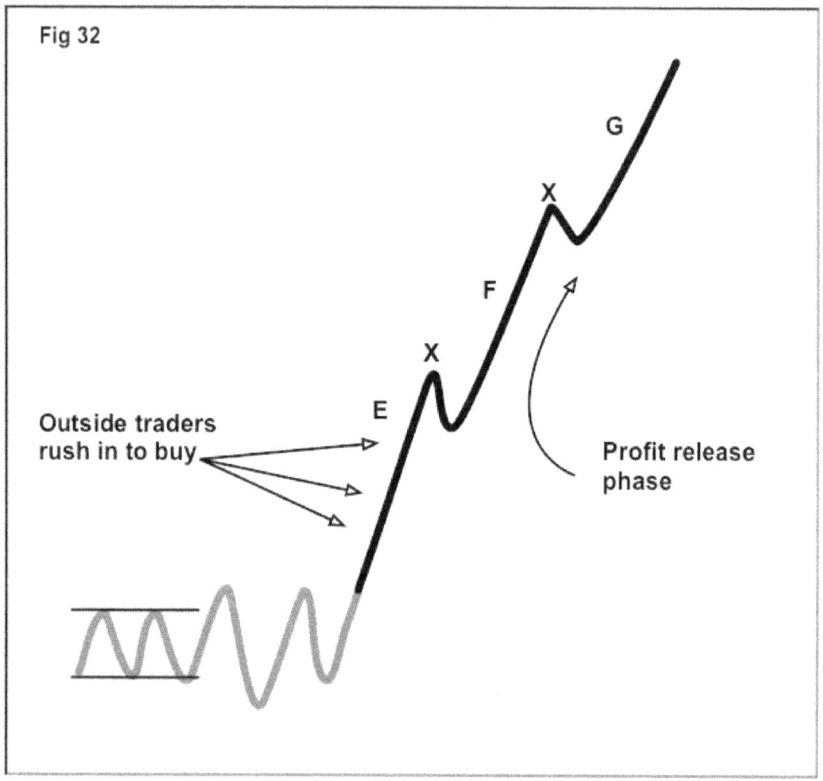

In Fig 32, the market makes a clear and defined move (E), the outside traders will see this and will immediately start to buy the market. The market makers who bought earlier and have a much lower average price will now sell some of their buy orders to the outsiders, thus releasing profits for themselves.

Looking at the chart, you will notice a series of small drop-backs. I have marked these with (X). These drop-backs are caused by the market makers profit release on this first rise. As the market makers willingly sell to the outsiders who are rushing in, they over sell to the demand, so demand from the outside is not enough, and thus the price retraces a little.

The market maker sees this and quickly buys back that which he over supplied on the rise. This again has the effect of pushing the market higher onto its next rise (F), encouraging yet more buyers for the market makers to release their accumulated buy orders to, and so onto (G)

WHERE IS A HIGH OR LOW?

It is said there is more money lost on predicting market high and lows than any other form of trading strategy. I believe this to be true and the reason I believe this is because traders use chart patterns and technical indicators to numerically measure something that is not based on numerical values.

However, there is a simple law which will always predict the end of any up move and the end of any down move. This law is one of profitability.

The market makers will only move a market up as long as they have buy orders to sell at a profit. They will only move a market down for as long as they have sell orders to profit from.

To take a market higher without any buy orders to sell at higher prices later on for profit is like a shop owner opening a store without anything to sell. Sure a few people may wander in but how long will they hang around?

Well, this brings us full circle.

The three phases of the market makers business model and the three strategies which drive the model.

Do you remember my statement a while ago regarding do you need a strategy?

Here it is again.

> Do you need to devise a personal trading strategy if the market makers BUSINESS MODEL is as consistent as the rising sun and it provides you with a method to continually profit?

Does this now make sense? I hope so because once you understand the market makers business model and then you understand the strategy which is attached to each phase of that model, you have a complete understanding of the market.

Once you can observe each phase, along with each strategy for each phase being played out, you only have to wait for the profit release phase and then join it.

This is the MARKET MAKERS strategy, and this is now YOUR strategy.

I will go as far as saying that if you operate outside of the market makers strategy, then you are 95% certain to become a victim of it.

A side note*

It always confused and disappointed me somewhat when I looked a some of the negative reviews of the early release of this book. I could not at first work out why they would give it a poor rating where most were delighted. Gradually it became clear.

Some readers had bought the book for a PATTERN. They wanted me to show them a pattern on a chart where they could buy and sell. They wanted to look at FORM.

Because they started reading the book with that BELIEF that a chart pattern was what it was all about they simply did not see the wood for the trees. They read the book and remained blind to the COMPLETE trading solution that has been presented.

I remember one review saying "It's a pamphlet trying to sell software" despite me stating the software was not required to trade the method.

Fortunately, some of these readers contacted me, and I was able to get them to go back and analyze the contents of the book to discover just how powerful a method this is. Some, of course, did not contact and I can only hope they found out the truth of the contents by actual observation.

Anyway... Let's get back to it with the essential steps before entering any trade.

6

THE ESSENTIAL STEPS BEFORE ENTERING A TRADE

Before you enter any market, you should have a clearly defined outcome; you should have a plan for when you are going to get out.

THE MARKET MAKERS method provides you with a consistent, reliable trading method. Three never changing phases, each with never changing strategies that make up the market makers business model.

THE METHOD IS an unbeatable formula for success.

BUT, we can reduce this formula even further by saying that all we really need to know is what the market maker is accumulating?

IF BUYS THEN the market is ultimately going to go up from the accumulation area. If sells then the market is ultimately going to go down from the accumulation area.

WHEN WE DISCOVER the contents of the box, we have discovered the future direction of the market.

The essential steps before entering a trade are:

1. Discover the contents of the box (buy or sell orders)
2. Discover when the market maker has accumulated all he wants
3. Work out your exit
4. Join the profit release

IN THE EARLY STAGES, many traders try to join the profit release without working out the contents of the box. The problem with this is that without the contents of the box being known to the best of your ability, you are entering a profit release phase you have no idea to which side (buys or sells) profit will be released.

THE MOST IMPORTANT AREA ON THE CHART

Many traders believe or are led to believe, that the most important area on a chart is the live edge. This misinformation causes the mind of the trader to be drawn to watching the live prices flicking up and down on the chart. This constantly moving price will be toying with the trader's beliefs about whether the market will ultimately move higher or lower. By becoming fixated on the live price movement, the trader becomes distracted from what is the single most important area on any chart in any market. That being the accumulation area, the box. Without the box there is nothing, there is no substance, and there can be no understanding of future market direction.

The market is driven by constant profit seeking and it all starts in the box because the box is the area of accumulation of either buy or sell orders.

The accumulation of buy orders will mean by default that the market will rise. Likewise, the accumulation of sell orders will mean by default that the market will fall.

Given this fact, based upon the absolute need for profit, the trader should be quite clear on his one solitary task if he is to make a success of his trading.

All traders need to focus on is the one solitary task of discovering the contents of the box. If we force our minds to stay connected to the box, then we stay connected to the actions of the market makers.

If we stay connected to the actions of the market makers, we will be able to read their actions which will logically draw us to discovering whether they are accumulating buy or sell orders. Once discovered, it is but a short step to joining in on the market makers profit release phase for ourselves.

THE PSYCHOLOGY OF TRADING

There continues to be much written about trading psychology, and while I agree a lot of it is written in good faith, I also believe that trading psychology is nowhere near as important as traders are led to believe it is.

The basis of trading psychology is centered around the premise that trading causes psychological interference with trading decisions and if this interference were not present, successful trading would emerge. What I would like to suggest is that interference is a normal part of the decision-making process where there are variables to consider.

The decision to buy a loaf of bread or not does not conjure up much of a decision making process. However, if we overlay this decision with a few more variables such as brown or white, whole grain or processed, large or small, things start to become a little more complex but certainly nothing that would likely cause a psychological issue. However, if our decision might make us sick in some unknown way, then we are likely to introduce an element of psychology into the mix.

Trading is unlikely to make us sick but it does have unknown outcomes, and it's these unknowns which set up the foundation for what many call 'the psychology of trading.'

Most of these unknowns stem from pattern trading. Pattern trading, as the name suggests involves searching for repeating patterns resulting in repeating outcomes. The logic of this goes something like this:

Once the trader has known repeatable results, the psychological interference will evaporate.

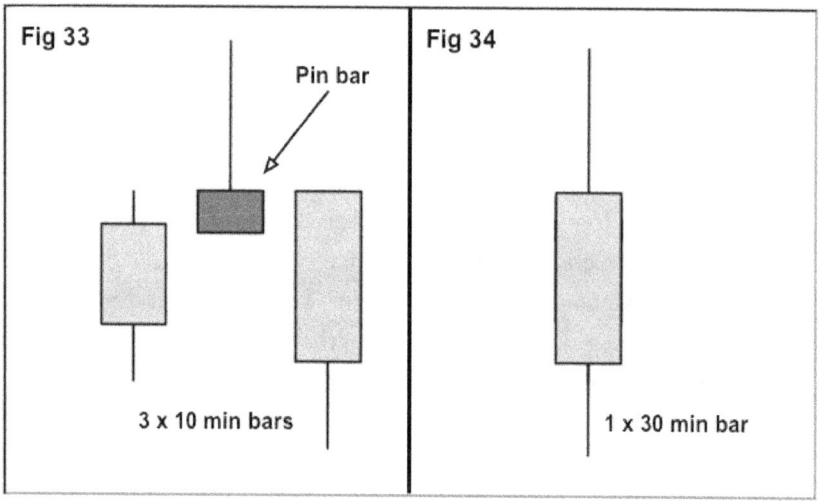

As a simple example of a repeatable outcome, let us use a popular chart pattern seen here in Fig 33. This pattern has been created from 3 x 10-minute bars of market activity. This three bar pattern contains a popular single bar called a pin bar.

The pin bar in Fig 33 is pointing upward. As traders who look for pin bars will tell you, the market is likely to fall from this point. All good sound advice, if it were true and if it were consistent. The problem with trading the FORM presented on the chart is that this form is completely arbitrary. We can change the form by simply changing the time frame.

Fig 34 is the same 3 x 10 minutes of market activity but in a single 30 minutes bar. Same data, same information, different form. The fact is that any bar pattern appearance can be changed by nothing more than the changing of the time frame.

Our pin bar trader will for sure have many and varied explanations about why 'some' of these bars are accurate, and others are not but when all said and done every pattern can be manipulated by a simple time frame change.

Furthermore, since the market is a constant stream of prices, where does one start or stop in any time frame?

The human mind will always see an unknown variable as a potential threat and the more times the mind is exposed to a threat, the greater the threat will be perceived. Trading the markets under threat, real or perceived is untenable for the mind and will result in failure.

Traders, in an attempt to rid themselves of what they now perceive as their problem, will engage in the process of strategy design in a bid to remove the psychological element of placing a trade. These strategic plans are often centered around automated systems requiring no human input.

Automated systems, while widely advertised and continually promoted, are a pipe dream and if you are up to the hike, will only be found at the end of a rainbow.

Trading psychology has evolved into a complete industry centered around traders having personal issues preventing them from achieving success. The truth is, in almost all cases, these so called personal issues are based squarely on having to make decisions based on patterns which can be created at will but also produce inconsistent results.

The result is huge numbers of traders believing there is something wrong with them, something wrong with the way they trade.

The solution is to trade from a position of understanding the reason behind every market move. Once you understand the market makers business model, once you see the model in action, you will be able to trade the markets without any psychological overlay.

YOUR ONE SINGLE TASK AS A TRADER

As a trader, your single task is to discover the plot, to discover the contents of the box. Are the market makers accumulating buy or sell orders? The answer to that question is achieved by asking 'what if' questions of the market. These what if questions keep your mind focused on what you need to have your attention focussed on, and they form the basis of reading the market.

Let's look at this from the angle of a movie plot (some better than others of course). As we watch the movie, the plot unfolds, there are a few twists and turns on the way to keep us hooked, but bit by bit the villain is revealed, the plot discovered, and the movie reaches its climax.

Entering a trade with the intention of making a profit from a market move, follows much the same path as the movie.

First, we have the plot set up, which is the accumulation. Next, we may get some misleading information which sends us off in the wrong direction; this is like the stop taking moves we have covered.

Finally, we see where the plot is heading in the movie, which is likened to when we see the direction of the profit release.

Each part of this trading story is of vital importance to you. Imagine trying to guess the outcome of a movie without knowing the plot? Without ever knowing the contents of the box?

By this stage, you are likely to understand the accumulation area and the placing of stops, which are harvested by the market markers when required. It is also hoped that by this stage you will begin to see this is a never ending story in the constant cycle for profits, a never ending story you can profit from.

LOSING AND DISCOVERING THE PLOT

Without a doubt, we all sometimes lose the plot of a movie. This might happen when we miss a vital part, or even something as simple as not hearing an actor's line, or misinterpreting a line. However, if we keep watching the movie gradually we will get the 'ah ha' moment, and we will be right back on track and feel more confident about where the movie is heading.

Trading the markets is the same. Every market movement starts off with a covert operation of either the accumulation of either buy or sell orders. Our job is to uncover the covert operation and to do this; we need to ask the following questions continually:

1. Have I defined the accumulation area?
2. Where have the outside traders likely placed their stop orders?
3. Is the market makers try to take out the stops to wrong foot the outside traders, where will this take place?
4. If the market makers stop taking takes place, what will I expect to see?

If the market makers stop is to accumulate buys, we can safely assume the contents of the accumulation is buy orders and from then on, we can plan our market entry strategy.

The answer to 1 does not provide you with a trading opportunity, neither does the answer to 2, 3, and 4; these are just the planning factors to focus on while we await the emergence of the signal that the profit release phase is under way.

The path to making a trading decision is discovering the plot and the plot in this case, is the accumulation of either buy orders or sell orders.

The emergence of the profit release phase is the result of the accumulation cycle, and this emergence will be our indication to join in with the market makers activities.

When you stop and think about this for a moment, you can say that all your analysis at any moment is 100% focussed on discovering the contents of the accumulation box.

WHEN THINGS GO WRONG

In life things go wrong, we make wrong decisions, say the wrong things and take the occasional wrong turn on the highway. Trading is the same, and we need to understand what is going on and how to deal with it.

The knowledge to know when to exit a market is every bit as important as the knowledge to enter the market. Few traders really master the skill of when to exit trades which are not working out as planned. Instead, they will move stop loss orders and then just wait in the hope the trade works out. What happens is that over time they lose on these trades and these losses mount up.

Understanding this inability to pull out of trades, which are not working out can be likened to you standing toe to toe in a boxing ring. The other boxer is constantly hitting you on the end of your nose. Soon you try to dodge the punches. What are you trying to do? You may think you are trying to dodge the punch but what you are really doing is avoiding pain. This pain avoidance is a normal human reaction, but it is the reaction of an amateur boxer; a professional boxer will sometimes leave himself open to a punch and take some pain because, at that moment, he can also be the most dangerous to his opponent.

As a trader, you need to learn how to counter punch and doing so will often involve closing a trade even at a loss (take the punch on the nose) and then waiting for the next opportunity to develop.

If you have been trading for any degree of time, you will likely already understand about taking punches on the nose. Most likely you will also understand if you are completely honest with yourself, you 'somehow' know when a trade you are in is going bad. Often rather than dealing with the punch, you sidestep this by either moving your stop loss or by going into a hope mode.

Hope mode is when you intuitively know you are not in a good trading position but rather than doing something about it you sit staring at your charts in the hope it will all turn out good. You are likely just delaying the inevitable pain.

If you are a new trader, I urge you to cultivate the recognition of the very human sensation of hope. When you recognize this feeling within yourself, it is time to take that punch on the nose as a loss and get out of the market so you can return to the task of discovering the contents of the box.

Once you are in a trade, your ability to continually question the contents of the box diminishes as you focus on your belief being correct.

Most likely by this stage, you are thinking about getting ready to make a start. You are maybe thinking you can understand the ideas so far and now all you have to do is turn on a chart and start picking some trades.

However, if you were to start now, chances are you will either fail or achieve mediocre trading results. On the other hand, if you are prepared to take a leap of faith in what I am about to try to convey to you, then your trading world and quite possibly your life as a result of your trading is unlikely ever to be the same again.

7

THE SUBCONSCIOUS MIND

Experience over many years as a trader has taught me just how powerful the subconscious mind can have on a trader. This effect is far too significant to overlook.

I WOULD LIKE to tell you a story about a girl and a lollipop.

IN MY 30'S I trained as a hypnotherapist and was consulted by a woman who suffered from an excessive hand washing affliction.

This hand washing had begun following a seemingly incidental car accident which had left her rather upset. Over the following years, her condition worsened to the point where her hands would crack and bleed from the washing. Her life and family were deeply affected by her problem, but despite all her efforts to rationalize and deal with what was happening, she could not break the cycle and stop the obsessive behavior.

WORKING TOGETHER, my client arrived at an incident in her childhood that resulted in the emergence of the affliction. She remembered standing beside her mother at the kitchen sink enjoying a cherry lollipop when she was told to tie her shoelace. The little girl reached up, placed the lollipop on the work surface and bent down to tie her lace. As she did, the sweet rolled onto the floor, at which point she picked it up and put it in her mouth. Unexpectedly the mother shouted and slapped the little girl, shaking her violently as she explained with great drama all the terrible things germs could do to her.

AN EMOTIONAL EVENT of huge proportion had occurred, and it was locked away in the child's subconscious, only to emerge years later at the prompting of the stress caused by the car accident.

AS HER MIND struggled to deal with the car accident, it latched on to the childhood incident, prompted by the similar emotions that the two quite different events caused.

THE INCIDENT DESCRIBED above might not seem, to an adult, to be significant enough to result in the condition suffered by my client but when it occurred, the subconscious had to handle it as best it could for the child's protection.

IN SUCH SITUATIONS, the subconscious often locks the memory and the emotional content of the experience away, where they cannot readily be accessed. The idea of "locking away" is important to your understanding of the following graphic examples.

IN THE ORDINARY day to day environment, any task from picking up a coffee cup to negotiating a flight of stairs is conducted using the experience as a model.

All these experiences are recorded in our subconscious mind available for instant retrieval without conscious awareness. The subconscious is a complex mechanism and associations between events are often much less straightforward than one might expect.

DAY TO DAY TASKS AND THE SUBCONSCIOUS

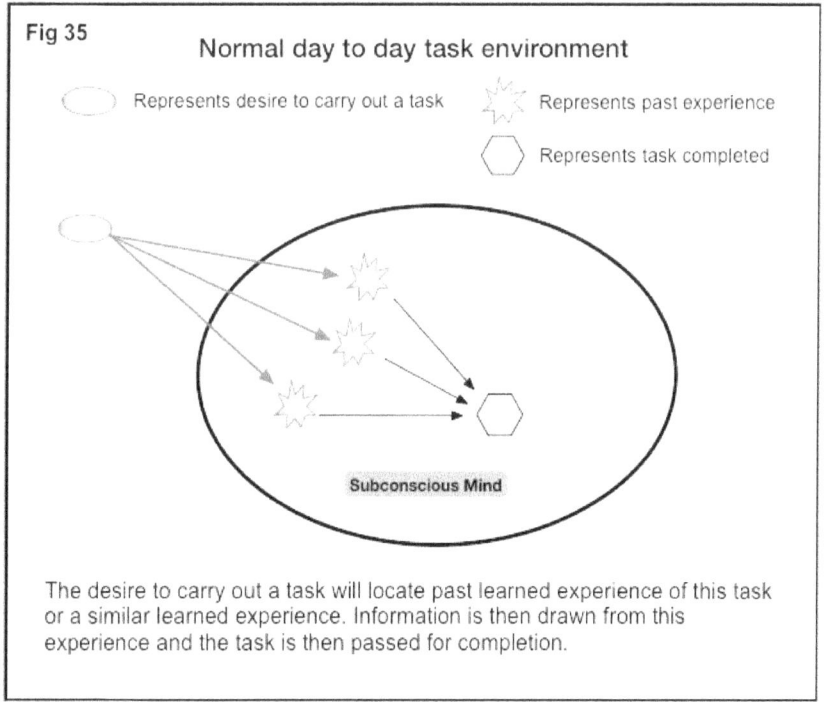

Fig 35 — Normal day to day task environment

○ Represents desire to carry out a task
✳ Represents past experience
⬡ Represents task completed

Subconscious Mind

The desire to carry out a task will locate past learned experience of this task or a similar learned experience. Information is then drawn from this experience and the task is then passed for completion.

Fig 35 shows the normal day to day task environment. This model allows us to operate very efficiently. We do not have to think about how to pick up a coffee cup; how to bring it to our lips, how to prevent spilling or how to put it down.

We simply carry out the tasks on 'autopilot' response. These auto responses are like well-worn paths; it's very hard to deviate from them. Just try using the opposite hand to the one you usually use, and you'll see your actions are not nearly so smooth and automatic.

Now let's carry this forward to the trading environment.

PAPER TRADING VERSES LIVE TRADING

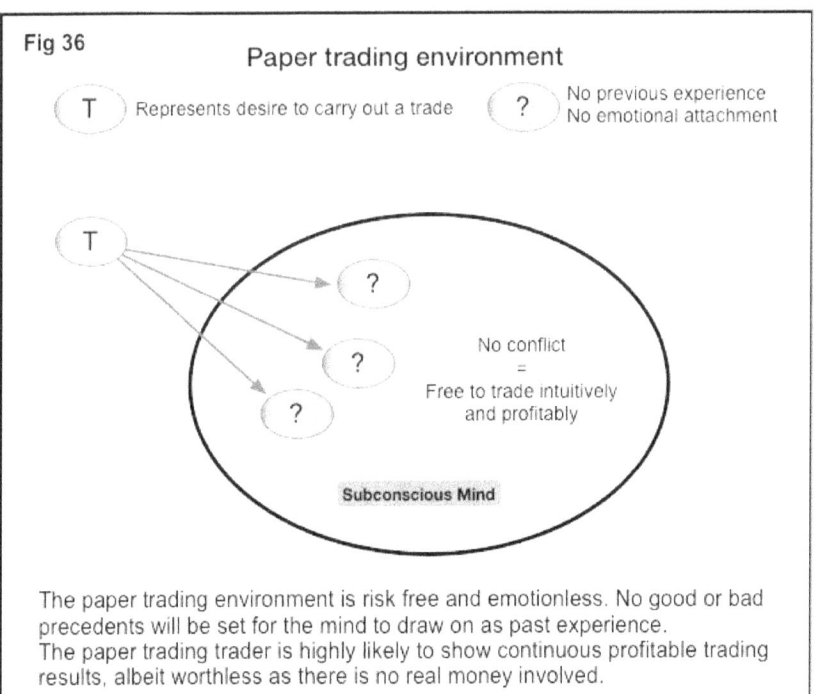

In Fig 36 (T) represents the desire to carry out a trade, in the context of a paper trading environment.

The mind scans rather like a radar screen for a previous experience with the components it seeks. As there is no real emotion in the paper trading environment, the mind finds little, if anything, to question carrying out the trade. This results in a fast, INTUITIVE action.

As increasing paper trades are carried out, the response to paper trading gets increasingly intuitive and uncomplicated. Traders in this environment are often able to produce outstanding results, which convince them that the time is right to do it for real!

The Live Trading Environment

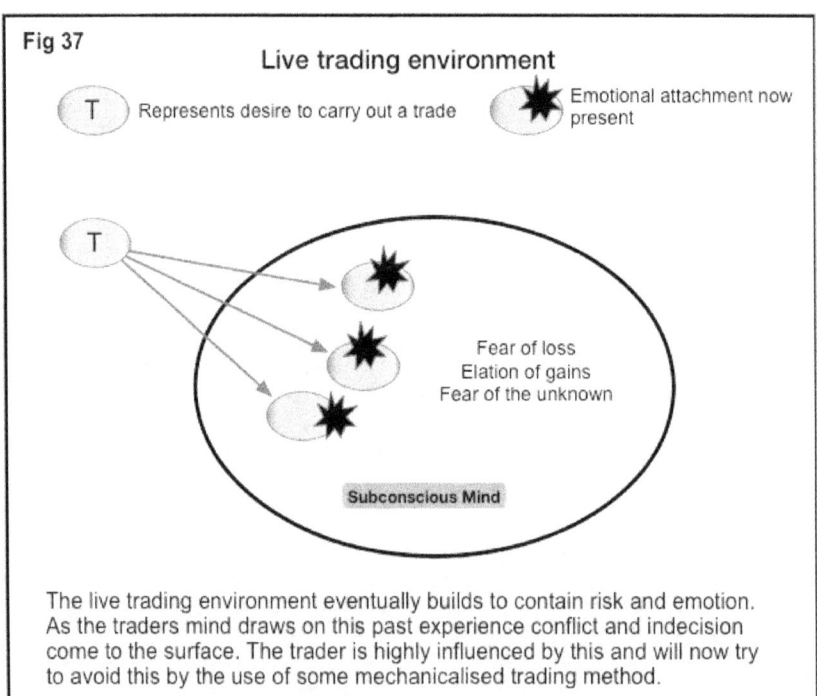

Fig 37 shows the desire to carry out the live trade the same as paper trading. Again the trader's mind is scanning through memories, searching for a comparable experience against which to judge his current situation.

Now, however, emotion is present, completely altering the trader's mental environment and because no two events are ever the same in trading, he will not find a suitable event to serve as a model for his behavior.

The mind only has emotional content on which to form the basis of a search. In other words, it will automatically begin to scan for memories associated with similar emotions to those felt at the time of trading.

As the trader is now trading live, the trader's current emotion is uncertainty, and a degree of fear and the subconscious mind will locate memories associated with these same feelings. Invariably, the memory of a fearful event is located, resulting in associating trading with a fear response. This association at first will be subtle, almost imperceptible.

The next time the trader moves towards placing at trade, the mind will automatically navigate to the association of fear. This neural pathway in mind is reinforced every time the traders actions a trade. The effects are compounded over time just like the hypnotist compounds suggestions to make them more effective. Eventually if left unchecked the trader will be unable to trade without the feeling of fear being triggered.

Decisions taken in a fearful state of mind do not produce good results. Most frequently, they cause traders to enter the market in completely the wrong direction, causing a loss and thus compounding the fearful situation.

The subconscious, does all it can to prevent the trader from experiencing negative emotions, to the extent of pushing him towards failure and removing him from the stressful environment altogether.

Over time, psychological paths to negative emotions will become deeper and deeper. The trader who finds himself in this position becomes irrational in his trading behavior. This situation often resulting in an endless search for a means to escape inner conflict and turmoil, from the latest software fad to esoteric trading guidance.

Successful traders need to engage in a trading method which allows them to take their decisions unemotionally, bypassing the subconscious association between trading and fear. This method should always be the same, and if the trader adheres to it, it will function in an emotion-free way, which does not admit the problematic elements of fear association and unnecessary failure.

Recognising the power inherent in the subconscious is an important step to take in neutralizing its potential to damage your trading success.

The market makers business model never changes, so once the trader learns this, there will be repeatable known outcomes.

If you are already trading and find yourself with any of the symptoms explained, then a period away from the market is certainly very important as is the study and application of the market makers business model as a trading solution when you return.

8
THE WRAP-UP

It is said traders fail for a variety of reasons, including risking too much money, lacking an exit strategy, a dearth of numeracy and the failure to understand risk. After my 20 plus years in this business, I have to disagree.

I BELIEVE traders fail because this is how the market makers business model is designed. This is their business, not ours. If we trade with the tools and data, they freely provide we will be forever under their shadow. We will forever be victims of their manipulation.

Losses

DEALING with losses is a matter of adjusting your attitude. Losing traders believe losses are a reflection of their personality and lose self-esteem every time they lose money. They think failure is liable to continue, coupled with the idea they must never lose while trading.

WINNING traders accept losses are part of the business and do not assume a loss is a reflection of their personalities. A certain amount of loss in trading is inevitable, and this has to be accepted. Winning traders tend to focus on what is important, like trading skills and developing a quality trade mentality.

LEARN TO ASK yourself whether your trade is consistent with the rules of the method. Ask yourself whether you are happy with the way it was carried out and whether you would carry out another trade in the same manner.

The ability to answer "yes" to these questions demonstrates you are building a quality trade mentality, demonstrates you are focussing on the overall content of trading and not on individual trades.

Winning traders know that while the market is controlled and manipulated, they can join the professionals in making a profit through using the market makers business for their own benefit.

MANY TRADERS USE words with painful overtones when talking about getting stopped out. 'My stop was hit, 'knocked out again' 'booted out, 'I took a hit' etc. The reason for this is because they associate financial loss with pain and as we know the human mind will do anything it can to avoid pain. By associating loss with pain, we will naturally try to avoid loss. Avoiding loss for a trader might be a delay in closing a trade which is not working out, or just waiting with bated breath as the market edges ever closer to the stop loss order. You see there is always the 'hope' the trade may work out and your stop loss will not be 'hit' better to wait and see eh! Just in case it's a winner.

WHAT HAPPENS MORE OFTEN than not is the trader becomes fixated on his stop loss order, his pain avoidance mechanism takes over, and nothing else matters. Now the trader is blind, blind to reading what is perhaps emerging as the perfect trading opportunity.

CLOSING a trade which is not working out will often mean you are taking a financial loss and you need to know if you are associating this with pain or at least giving energy to the thought of pain. If you have been trading for anytime, you can carry out a simple test that will determine how vulnerable you are to getting caught into the trap of pain avoidance.

HAVE you ever found yourself in a trade which was not going your way? On and on it drags almost teasing the price where you have placed your stop loss order. Cast your mind back to that time. Did you ever find yourself 'wanting' to be stopped out so the pain could be over? If you have experienced these feelings, they are a measure of how you view loss and how you have maybe have linked this losing to pain.

HERE IS a three part quick solution for when you find yourself in this situation Although this solution is easy to describe and understand, it is not so easy to implement because of our basic instinct to what we perceive as a loss.

1. Listen to your instincts when a trade is not going your way
2. Close the trade regardless of win or loss
3. Walk away from the screen for at least 20 minutes

IF YOU DO NOT MOVE AWAY from the screen at this point you will become mentally anchored into battle with a crippling thought process; should I, or should I have not closed that trade? This mental anchoring will cause a negative reaction to taking a loss, which will then be anchored to the next time you intrinsically know you should close a trade. Over time this will cause a negative feedback loop which will continue to do damage as long as it exists.

WELL, that's it here you are at the end with the potential of a new beginning. Of course you may not believe trading can be this simple. If you are the possessor that 'belief' then I would ask you to do what the wright brothers did when they decided man could fly. They chose to ignore what others believed and look at it from a different perspective in doing so they changed the world forever in an instant.

JUST ONE MORE THING.

9

PAT SOFTWARE & TRAINING

At the beginning of this book, I explained how I met the computer programmer and how we worked together to create software. This software was only ever intended to be my personal software. The last thing I wanted was to develop another business with employees - hey that is what I escaped from when I became a trader.

However, over the years I did share my software with traders I had worked with. For some of them, it was as they said 'the best thing since sliced bread' for others it was just not something they felt comfortable using so they stuck with traditional candle charts and also become very successful.

What I am trying to convey here is that PAT software is a TOOL that was designed for myself to trade the market makers method. This tool is essential for some and not so for others.

I realize that I could be a better 'salesman' and say...

"Hey, you MUST have PAT software to trade the market makers method."

The problem is, that would be a lie, and everything that I have explained in the book would then be a lie. The market makers method is the market makers BUSINESS MODEL. That model exists INDEPENDENT of you, I or any software.

So should you try my software? Well, that is your call, BUT I would urge you to start without it. I would urge you to prove to yourself that everything I have explained here can be observed in all markets in all time frames.

Working with me

Training is something that I wholeheartedly believe in. Good training can shave years off your learning curve. Unfortunately, the learning curve for a trader can be very costly if you don't get things right pretty quickly. I have seen many a good trader quit this business because time and or money needlessly ran out.

To this end, I have created what I consider to be the ultimate trader training course. You get to spend over 6 hours with me on video as I explain everything in this book and much more.

Should you be skeptical of trader training courses? Yes!

My training has over the years been stolen, reworked, repackaged and sold to unsuspecting victims. One 'guru' made more than 3 million dollars by concocting a dead broker story and saying that the market makers make M and W patterns (FORM) and all you have to do is trade the M and W.

By now I hope you realize the folly of such things and hopefully you have not been 'caught' too many times with your wallet open.

If you would like to train with me, then I welcome you as a student. I am confident that after you get involved with my training course and experience learning from the original discoverer of the market makers method you will be more than delighted with your results.

If you like the idea of us working together, then please drop by my website and say hello. I look forward to hearing from you.

WE CAN CATCH up at www.learningtotrade.com, or you can go direct to the training site and check out the options there.

HTTP://MARKET-MAKERS-METHOD.THINKIFIC.COM

ALL THE VERY BEST from my family to yours

Martin Cole

PS If you have enjoyed this book and found it of value, please drop me a line and let me know and don't forget that a review on Amazon goes a long way towards helping others.

I believe it's important to share the skills we have in life with others so that they may shorten and better enjoy their journey.

HTTP://WWW.LEARNINGTOTRADE.COM/KINDLEMMB.HTM

OTHER BOOKS BY MARTIN COLE

THE BILLIONAIRE AND THE BACKPACKER

Imagine starting your life over again but with all the life experience of today. It would be a dizzying journey of success and achievement that would leave those around you standing in awe. They would have no clue where your wisdom, foresight and abilities came from. A sought-after person you would be for sure.

The Billionaire and the backpacker story is inspired by true events. The messages woven through the story will reveal to you the potential for a restart - a reboot of your life. It's a book that could quite possibly change your life!

The billionaire and the backpack takes you on a captivating journey from the sidewalks of New York to the Peruvian jungle where an ancient ceremony revealed that nothing is without meaning, consequence and maybe even destiny.

Take this book home tonight and expose yourself to the very real possibility of a life changing story.

How to not be just another egg in the trading game

This book contains often overlooked or just plain ignored facts about trading. Traders who have read this book with twenty plus years under their belt and still come away with some revelations that has had a dramatic effect on their trading.

—- Image Below —

ABOUT MARTINS OTHER BOOKS

Martin believes that everyone has a core purpose to their life and discovering this purpose is of the utmost importance. Out of purpose comes passion and there is little that contains more power than a person living their life with these two forces combined.

Martin hopes that through his books readers may catch glimpses of their own lives and discover that their life can be every bit as empowered as the characters in the story.

Martin uses skillful story telling to invite you into a world of exciting possibilities for personal growth, successful living, and a joyful life.

Please drop by and say hello at:
www.martincole.com

www.ingramcontent.com/pod-product-compliance
Lightning Source LLC
Chambersburg PA
CBHW071158240526
45470CB00017B/292